D1537714

BYTE's Windows Programmer's Cookbook

About the CD-ROM

Disc Contents:

All of the programs listed in this book can be found on this CD-ROM. They are Windows 3.1 and/or Windows NT programs. The CD is organized in directories that correspond to the chapters in the book. Appendix B in the book shows all files in alphabetical order with brief descriptions.

The CD has a program named WINCOOK1.EXE that displays lists of all the files with descriptions and the Osborne/McGraw-Hill catalog. We encourage you to use this program. To access it, simply execute the program from the Program Manager (see the Introduction to the book if you need help installing this file). The WINCOOK1 program requires a minimal MPC system. Other files on the disk require only a Windows 3.1, 2MB RAM, VGA system.

Using the CD:

To open the files, we recommend that you use the program WinZip, which is located in the root directory on the CD. Remember to register this and the other shareware on the CD that you decide to use. The programs are provided on the CD for your convenience. We have tested the programs and have concluded that they perform their function well. However, because they are shareware, we do not offer technical support for the individual programs, nor can we vouch for their robustness. Each shareware program includes a screen informing you of registration fees and technical support policies. You can also locate the shareware developers for support by looking in the Hack Facts boxes throughout the book. Also, remember to read the README files.

For more instructions on the use of the CD, see the "More on the CD" section in the Introduction or better yet, see Appendix A, "Installation of the CD-ROM." If you find any problems with the CD media or with the file structure on your CD, call Osborne/McGraw-Hill at 800/227-0900.

WARNING: BEFORE OPENING THE DISC PACKAGE, CAREFULLY READ THE TERMS AND CONDITIONS OF THE FOLLOWING CD-ROM WARRANTY.

Disc Warranty

This software is protected by both United States copyright law and international copyright treaty provision. You must treat this software just like a book, except that you may copy it into a computer to be used and you may make archival copies of the software for the sole purpose of backing up our software and protecting your investment from loss. By saying, "just like a book," Osborne/McGraw-Hill means, for example, that this software may be used by any number of people and may be freely moved from one computer location to another, so long as there is no possibility of its being used at one location or on one computer while it is being used at another. Just as a book cannot be read by two different people in two different places at the same time, neither can the software be used by two different people in two different places at the same time (unless, of course, Osborne's copyright is being violated).

Limited Warranty

Osborne/McGraw-Hill warrants the physical compact disc enclosed herein to be free of defects in materials and workmanship for a period of sixty days from the purchase date. If Osborne/McGraw-Hill receives written notification within the warranty period of defects in materials or workmanship, and such notification is determined by Osborne/McGraw-Hill to be correct, Osborne/McGraw-Hill will replace the defective disc.

The entire and exclusive liability and remedy for breach of this Limited Warranty shall be limited to replacement of defective disc and shall not include or extend to any claim for or right to cover any other damages, including but not limited to, loss of profit, data, or use of the software, or special, incidental, or consequential damages or other similar claims, even if Osborne/McGraw-Hill has been specifically advised of the possibility of such damages. In no event will Osborne/McGraw-Hill's liability for any damages to you or any other person ever exceed the lower of the suggested list price or actual price paid for the license to use the software, regardless of any form of the claim.

OSBORNE, A DIVISION OF McGRAW-HILL, INC., SPECIFICALLY DISCLAIMS ALL OTHER WARRANTIES, EXPRESS OR IMPLIED, INCLUDING BUT NOT LIMITED TO, ANY IMPLIED WARRANTY OF MERCHANTABILITY OR FITNESS FOR A PARTICULAR PURPOSE. Specifically, Osborne/McGraw-Hill makes no representation or warranty that the software is fit for any particular purpose, and any implied warranty of merchantability is limited to the sixty-day duration of the Limited Warranty covering the physical disc only (and not the software), and is otherwise expressly and specifically disclaimed.

This limited warranty gives you specific legal rights; you may have others which may vary from state to state. Some states do not allow the exclusion of incidental or consequential damages, or the limitation on how long an implied warranty lasts, so some of the above may not apply to you.

BYTE's Windows Programmer's Cookbook

L. John Ribar

Osborne **McGraw-Hill**

Berkeley · New York · St. Louis · San Francisco
Auckland · Bogotá · Hamburg · London · Madrid · Mexico City · Milan
Montreal · New Delhi · Panama City · Paris · São Paulo
Singapore · Sydney · Tokyo · Toronto

Osborne **McGraw-Hill**
2600 Tenth Street
Berkeley, California 94710
U.S.A.

For information on software, translations, or book distributors outside of the U.S.A., please write to Osborne McGraw-Hill at the above address.

BYTE's Windows Programmer's Cookbook

Copyright © 1994 by McGraw-Hill, Inc. All rights reserved. Printed in the United States of America. Except as permitted under the Copyright Act of 1976, no part of this publication may be reproduced or distributed in any form or by any means, or stored in a database or retrieval system, without the prior written permission of the publisher, with the exception that the program listings may be entered, stored, and executed in a computer system, but they may not be reproduced for publication.

1234567890 DOC 9987654

ISBN 0-07-882037-5

Information has been obtained by Osborne **McGraw-Hill** from sources believed to be reliable. However, because of the possibility of human or mechanical error by our sources, Osborne **McGraw-Hill**, or others, Osborne **McGraw-Hill** does not guarantee the accuracy, adequacy, or completeness of any information and is not responsible for any errors or omissions or the results obtained from use of such information.

"... dedicated to the proposition
that all men are created equal ..."

—Abraham Lincoln

Contents at a Glance

Contents

Acknowledgments

In putting this book together, I think I owe the biggest debt to those many shareware authors who have filled the world with their wares. I'm one, too, but if I was the only one, you would never hear of shareware. I can't name them all, but if you've put out a good shareware program, I'm talking about you!

As always, the staff at Osborne/McGraw-Hill is a joy to work with. This time, the cast included Jeff Pepper, Vicki Van Ausdall, Rachel Howes, Janet Walden, Jan Jue, Pat Mannion, and Valerie Robbins. Thanks go to them all for their support, encouragement, and flexibility. Special thanks to Tay Vaughan and Walnut Creek Software for putting together the CD.

Finally, I need to thank my wife, Deborah, and my children, Louis, Jamie, Michael, and Leah. The kids put in a lot of time at my office while Mom was working and I was writing, so they deserve a big round of applause.

Introduction

Isn't this great? You have a book here with a CD-ROM in it! It's full of software that you, as a programmer, can make use of right away.

How can this be? How can you get a CD-ROM full of software for merely the price of a book? Is this some sort of put-on, with a hidden camera lurking behind the book racks? Have you died and gone to a better place?

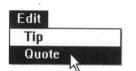

It's fun sitting at a terminal and letting the code flow.
—Gary Kildall

Nope. It's simple (to explain)! It's new (kinda)! It's exciting! It's called *shareware*, a form of software distribution in which the programmers and authors allow you to use their program for free, while you decide if it fits with your needs and desires. After that time, you either pay for the software, or stop using it.

Naturally, if you didn't like the program, you'd probably get rid of it anyway. But if you like the program, if it fills some need, if it is of use to you on a regular basis, then you should be prepared to pay for it.

Here's another surprise: shareware is priced much less than equivalent retail software! And I say "equivalent" because much shareware is as good, or even better, than the software you buy for inflated prices at stores.

But enough about the shareware concept for now; I'll tell you more about it in the first chapter. In fact, this is probably a good time to tell you what you can expect to find in this book and on the enclosed CD-ROM disc.

What We're Doing in Here

In Chapter 1, "Finding the Treasure Chest," we will discuss the locations in which these programmer's gems are found. This includes electronic services (CompuServe, America Online, and others), bulletin boards specializing in items of interest, and CD-ROMs containing prebuilt collections.

Chapter 2, "Programmers' Assistants," discusses those hard-to-be-without utilities available for Windows-based programmers. These are not specifically for programming, but they aid in the everyday happenings that a Windows programmer may face.

In Chapter 3, "Language-Free and Language-Specific," we'll discuss libraries, utilities, and programming-specific items that Windows programmers can use in their work. Generally, these are not related to a specific language or environment.

Next, Chapter 4, "Glass Houses," discusses code samples, programs, and libraries into which you may peer (source code included). These will naturally be related to a specific language or environment, but since source is included, all the examples are informative for nearly everyone.

People should be able to speak and breathe programs just like they talk now.

—Jaron Lanier

Chapter 5 is "Programmer's Day Off." I know, you probably don't know what that is (a day off, I mean). But in this chapter, toys and tools that have little to do with programming are discussed. Even Windows programmers need to blow off steam sometimes. This chapter presents a collection of games, screen images and blankers, and other paraphernalia that is bound to provide some provocative release time for programmers facing burnout or extinction.

In Chapter 6, we turn to the "Business Managers." Here, you'll learn about small-business programs that are very useful to Windows programmers and consultants. This includes time and billing software, and tools to make your program easier to sell for the big bucks (installation programs and tools to build excellent help utilities for your own applications).

In Chapter 7, the "Document Library," text files and related items are discussed. Very often, the information you need is hiding in a README file somewhere. I'll also discuss adding some pizzazz to your Program Manager for all these text files.

Chapter 8 is the real test for you. There, you'll get the feel of going online. I've saved the newest releases of shareware for you, and presented them alphabetically, just like you'd see on a BBS. Take some time to hunt through Chapter 8, there is all kinds of stuff in there. It could have all been placed in the first seven chapters, but then you wouldn't get the joy of discovery!

Actually, there is a great deal of software on this CD-ROM. There is even a special program designed just for this series. In Appendix A, I'll tell you how to install the disc and start using the programs as soon as possible.

Then, Appendix B lists the programs on the disc, sorted alphabetically for your quick perusal. Once you've been through this book at least once, and want to go back for a specific piece of software, the appendix will be a great reference.

Finally, in Appendix C, I'll give you some hints for becoming a shareware author/programmer yourself. Actually, throughout the book there are references to things I think would be nice; maybe I'll spark an idea with you, and you'll need Appendix C to get started.

Throughout the book several special features show up. "Hack Facts" boxes display brief background information for the program currently being discussed. If you want to find the description of a program quickly, look through the Hack Facts until you find the one you need. It's much, much faster than skimming the text.

Second, there are tips and quotes scattered about for your enjoyment. The tips generally relate to the program or topic being discussed. The quotes, on the other hand, are only there for fun. Please realize that "enjoyment" is the key word here, as some of the quotes are short, and may have different possible interpretations based on the original context. If you need to write a research paper, let me know, and I'll tell you the rest of the story!

Some Assembly Required

There isn't much that you need to do to use the programs on the disc. They are stored in directories, one for each chapter.

Most of the programs are stored in ZIP files. This is one type of file used throughout the bulletin board and shareware world to store a lot of files together in a compressed format. Because of this, you need a program to unZip, or decompress, or unarchive the files. There is a wonderful shareware program called WinZip, in the top-level directory of the CD-ROM, that you can use for this purpose.

Tip

If you are familiar with the use of PKZIP or PKUNZIP (from PKWare), you may also use these programs (it's just that WinZip runs under Windows, while PKUNZIP runs under DOS—you make the choice).

Once the files are unZipped, give them a try like any other new Windows program. I think you'll have a good time, so you better get started.

By the way, if you find other good shareware, let me know. You can reach me on CompuServe at 72002,2245, or on my BBS at (717) 854-0542. It's hard to keep up; there is a lot of new software coming out all the time. Shareware is one method of distribution where smaller companies and programmers can fill the world with their programs at little or no cost. Keep your eyes open—there is surely more to come!

More on the CD

The CD-ROM contains all the files described in the book. The CD is broken into directories that correspond to the chapters. The CD contains a program, WINCOOK1.EXE, that lists the files by chapter with brief descriptions.

You can execute the WINCOOK1.EXE file in several ways. For instance, let's say your CD drive letter is **e**. By selecting Run from the Program Manager File menu and typing

```
e:\wincook1.exe
```

at the Command Line, the program will execute.

If you plan to use WINCOOK1.EXE frequently, another option is to create an icon for the Program Manager.

Finally, you can execute WINCOOK1.EXE by selecting Open from the File Manager File menu, single-clicking on the OMHCAT folder, and double-clicking on WINCOOK1.EXE. The benefit to this approach is that you can view all files and directories on the CD from the File Manager before executing the program.

You can find the file lists by pressing the "This CD-ROM" button in this program. You then have your choice. You can look at the individual chapters in the menu or you can choose to look at *all* of the programs on the CD by selecting Appendix B. In either case, you will see the filenames and a very brief summary of each program.

Tip

You can also just look at the directories without even loading this CD program, but you won't have the benefit of the summaries.

The CD also contains information on all Osborne/McGraw-Hill books—under the "Catalog" button. You can search the catalog by title, author, or topic; just click on an entry for a description of the book. You can find information on how to buy books using the "Purchase" button.

How to Decompress the Files

Since most of the files are compressed on the disc, the following should assist you in making the programs available on your hard disk.

First, look for the file you want. If you read about a program that sounds interesting in the book, look at the "Hack Facts" box in the book, and jot down the name of the archive file you need. Usually, it will end with the three-letter extension ZIP. This means that all the files you need have been compressed into a single file—the Zip file.

To extract the files from the Zip file, use the WinZip program. This excellent program is described in Chapter 2 of the book and has been placed in the top-level directory of the CD-ROM for quick access. Simply start the program, press the "Open" button, and navigate through the directories until you find the file you need.

Knowledge is of two kinds; we know a subject ourselves, or we know where we can find information upon it.
—Samuel Johnson

Next, press the "Extract" button. You will again navigate through the directories, this time searching for a location in which to extract all the files from the Zip file. By the way, you can specify a new subdirectory, and WinZip will automatically create it before decompressing your Zip file.

Many of the programs on the CD-ROM also require the use of certain files, notably VBRUN100.DLL, VBRUN200.DLL, and VBRUN300.DLL. These are special files used by applications that have been written in Visual Basic. Because of their common use, these three files have also been placed in the top-level directory of your CD-ROM, rather than being included in every program Zip file. To use these files, simply copy them to your WINDOWS\SYSTEM directory. If you've worked with shareware before, you may already find that one or more of these files exist on your drive; don't worry, just keep the file with the latest (most current) date.

Don't forget, most of these programs are *shareware*, which means that you need to pay for them if you end up using them regularly. Rates are reasonable, and you already have fully functional demonstrations from which to make decisions. Help support the shareware concept, so that more of this excellent software can be created and distributed.

If you should have any problem with the CD-ROM, contact Osborne/McGraw-Hill at 800/227-0900.

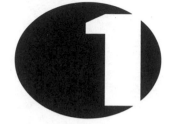

Finding the Treasure Chest

There you are sitting in front of your computer, having just finished a programming session that lasted most of the night. You need a break, but can't decide whether you'd prefer a round with a fast-action computer game, another Diet Coke, or a trip to an all-night coffee shop.

In a flash of inspiration, you pick up this book and try to see what's available to help you through the next programming session. You've always thought that there must be more to Windows programming than Hungarian notation, and that perhaps a book with a CD-ROM might be a good place to start finding out more.

Edit
Tip
Quote

At some point in the project you're going to have to break down and finally define the problem.

—Rick Cook

You're right, on both counts. This book is going to introduce you to some of the most exciting new software available for Windows, and all of the software mentioned here is on the enclosed CD-ROM disc.

In this chapter, you'll find out where this stuff comes from, why you haven't seen it at your local computer store, and where you can find even more. If you're already versed in electronic bulletin boards (BBSs), shareware, and CD-ROMs, skim quickly, so you can get into the program descriptions that begin in Chapter 2.

Any-Ware Will Do

The software discussed in this book isn't found in most computer stores. It goes by many names, even more than are listed here. After looking over the following list, you'll get the gist of it: this is software available for at least a trial use without any payment being made. As in, free.

Can you imagine asking your local Ford dealer if you could borrow a new Mustang for 21 days, and if you like it, you'll come back and pay for it? Probably not. How about asking Lotus to send you a copy of 1-2-3 for Windows (the latest revision, of course), without any prepayment, for a 10-day trial? Yeah, right.

but the programmers responsible for the software in this book (and much, much more that is available) really are giving you this free trial period. In some cases, the actual software is free too. (Think of all the Diet Cokes and trips to the coffee shop that'll buy you, not to mention...) How will you know what's what? For each program described in this book, I'll tell you whether or not payment is required.

Here are some of the names this type of software goes by:

Shareware
Shareware gets its name from the fact that the programmers want to *share* the software with you. Generally, it's *shareware* when you are expected to pay for the program if you like it and plan on using it. A shareware program is fully functional and will probably include messages, called annoyance screens (see "Begware" below), reminding you that you haven't yet paid for the program you're running. Of course, when you do finally pay, you'll get the latest version of the program (in case you've missed any), or at least a copy without the reminders! Often you will also get a manual and some additional features included in the paid-for registered version.

Begware
Begware is a version of shareware that uses an excessive number of messages to remind you to pay for your copy. Other than that, it should run fine—you may just lose your temper a little more often.

Crippleware

Crippleware is slightly different than shareware. With crippleware, you receive a program that has one of its major functions removed. For instance, a word processor that cannot print is crippled. Many companies think crippled versions of their software make excellent demonstrations. I, however, like to see whether a program's functions work properly, so a crippled version isn't always a good demonstration for me. I don't think there is any crippleware on the CD-ROM with this book, because there are enough crippled demo programs being sent out by the major software manufacturers and I didn't want to add to the glut. Here's a tip for you, though: each of those crippled demos comes on a diskette, often even more than one. Get my drift?

If you cannot convince them, confuse them.
—Harry S. Truman

Bannerware

Bannerware is software that is released to advertise other software. For instance, many of the great game programs available through the shareware channels offer you additional games once you register. So, bannerware is like the hook to catch you, and make you really want the other software the author sells. Don't get me wrong, I don't mind this approach; it just ends up costing me too much when I want all the other programs.

Freeware

This is the one you've been waiting for. No charge, no registration, but also no support. Freeware authors release their programs for your use, without expecting or requesting any payment. Often this is done just to keep the cost of support down (how much support can you expect for something you got free?). The authors, however, usually retain their copyright on the software, so you can't start selling it under your own name, raking in profits for something you didn't develop (not that anyone would ever consider such a thing).

Bookware

Bookware is one of my favorite types of software distribution. This and the other "wares" that follow are kinda freeware and kinda shareware. Freeware, because you usually don't get a lot of support even after you "pay." But, if you like the software, your payment doesn't involve cash! With bookware, for instance, all you pay is a book. Send the program author a science fiction paperback, or whatever form of literary nonsense they are interested in, and you are registered for the software. This is good for two reasons. First, it costs much less for you to send a five-dollar paperback than to pay for software at your local computer mart. Second, the book gives the programmer something to do besides program; this in turn allows fresh thoughts into their heads, and additional programs may follow. See what an influence you can be?

Postcardware

Some programmers producing shareware simply ask for a postcard from your local venue. This is their way to travel the world, I suppose, since many programmers won't do it in person. Be sure to send a good postcard; the better the response the programmer gets, the more inspired the software that will be produced. I can just imagine some poor programmer working away next to a wall full of postcards, all saying "This is a Generic Postcard from ...". Would this inspire and enlighten you?

Donorware

The programmers of donorware ask that if you want to continue to use their software, you make a donation to your favorite charity. Some authors request that you give a certain amount (the value of the program), while others don't set an amount. I know that this is a great thing for the programmers to do, donating all their time and efforts to charities. What I'm not sure of, though, is how they know they've been successful, and should continue to produce the software. I guess it probably doesn't matter.

*If you have too
many special cases,
you are doing it
wrong.*

—F. Jeff Stiles

Retail Software

We won't concern ourselves about this one for now. Buy retail software from your local computer dealer or one of the many fine mail-order dealers. There isn't any retail software on this CD-ROM, and there shouldn't be any available from the sources I'll discuss later. Actually, that isn't totally true; some shareware authors sell their registered (paid) versions in stores, offering the shareware version (don't forget those reminders!) as a demonstration, if you desire to try before you buy.

Public Domain Software

This is the most free, most unsupported, and most popular software for people with small budgets. Public domain software is released to anyone to use, copy, include in their own programs, or to do whatever seems appropriate. As opposed to freeware, public domain software does not carry a copyright, and there is never any payment expected by the original programmer or author.

Where Does this Stuff Come From?

Now that you have this book, you may be wondering how you can have access to all the great programs that are yet to be released. Do you need to buy updated versions of the book every month? Although I personally wouldn't mind, I think your bookshelves and budgets would soon tire from that type of purchase cycle.

Wherefore are these things hid?
—Shakespeare,
Twelfth Night

Instead, you can learn a lot from the programs included on this CD-ROM. For instance, many of the authors have their own electronic bulletin boards, where you can get the latest versions of their programs and often other programs too. There are also several major electronic services available, where you can obtain software from literally thousands of programmers in a single place. Let's talk about some of these now.

1

Bulletin Boards

So, what's an electronic bulletin board anyway? It's not just an electronic version of that piece of cork hanging on your wall. Think instead about the bulletin boards at your local grocery store or in the common areas of most college campuses. These are always full of random slips of paper, some nicely printed, others quickly scribbled. But anyone can place something on those boards, and once they do, it becomes available for everyone else to see.

Electronic bulletin boards follow the same concept. A bulletin board system (BBS) consists of a computer that is plugged into a phone line using a modem (the modem converts information from computer-ese to phone-ese). A special program runs on the BBS computer that allows people to call the modem (with their modems), and see listings of the files and messages that are available on the BBS. They can then download (copy from the BBS to their own computers) or upload (copy from their computer onto the BBS) files, post messages, etc. With some of the larger and more popular BBSs, there will usually be an annual fee arrangement. Sometimes, the more you pay, the more time you can spend connected to the BBS during a single day.

BBSs are a great tool for disseminating information. Of course, there are several BBS programs available, so for every BBS you call into, you may see different types of commands. Later, in Chapter 6, I'll talk about a shareware program that you can use to set up your own BBS.

Anyway, each BBS has its own specialty. There are thousands of BBSs throughout the United States, and indeed throughout the world. There are bulletin boards for nearly every interest, including the following:

Make sure you check anything you download from a BBS for viruses.

- Programming languages, such as ADA, C, C++, Pascal, and others
- Online games
- Stock prices
- Environmental issues and related support groups
- Support for specific software products
- Adventure games
- Children's programs, both entertainment and educational
- Religious discussions
- New car information
- Travel information
- Computer-aided drafting (CAD) support
- Consultant information
- News
- Weather information, including weather maps
- Genealogy research
- Desktop publishing

- Shareware distribution
- Legal issues
- Scuba diving
- Adult topics
- Bird watching
- Packet radio
- Engineering
- And many, many more

There are literally hundreds of specialties, and most BBS operators probably can say that their board is a little different than all the rest.

Hack Facts

Boardwatch Magazine

8500 W. Bowles Ave.,
Suite 210
Littleton, CO 80123
800/933-6038 Subscription
303/973-4222 BBS
$4.95 per issue,
$36 annual subscription

With all these bulletin boards in existence, finding the best ones can take a little work. There are, luckily, a few good places to start. First, pick up a copy of the latest edition of *Boardwatch* magazine. This is published monthly, and covers innumerable topics related to accessing online systems. Included is a list of popular BBS numbers, along with their topics of interest, locations, and other pertinent information. This list changes often, because bulletin boards come and go. More and more of the boards are also beginning to cover Windows-related topics, so it's worth checking out the latest list on a regular basis.

Also included in the magazine are descriptions of the various software packages used to run a BBS, discussions of new BBS technologies, and lots of interesting advertisements. By the way, this is also a good source of information about CD-ROMs; many bulletin board operators now use a CD-ROM drive so that the people calling into their BBS computer have access to lots of software. Naturally, a magazine like *Boardwatch* needs to discuss the best CD-ROMs.

Let's Get Started

Another good source of information about BBSs is from other BBSs; very often, there will be lists of BBS numbers available, which gives you even more numbers to call. Watch your phone bill, though. Even when calling late at night, it's easy to run up your phone bill faster than with your favorite 900 number! You can start by looking around on the Windows-related bulletin boards I've listed here.

Jádin Windows Extravaganza (Pennsylvania)	717/854-0542
PC-SIG BBS (California)	408/730-0502
PowerBBS Windows Support Line (New York)	516/822-7396
Public Brand Software BBS (Indiana)	317/856-2087
The Ultimate Windows BBS (Alberta, Canada)	403/539-6781
Windows Express (Virginia)	804/745-3743
Windows-R-Us (California)	619/944-7368

In addition, try calling the following vendors of shareware disks and ask for their latest catalogs. If you get on their mailing list, you'll be kept current with the latest shareware available. If you decide to order, they'll typically charge you a $3 or $5 fee which covers just the cost of the copying service, not the cost of the program. So remember that, just like the software included with this book, you must still pay for the program if you continue to use it.

CWI	800/777-5636
Public Brand Software	800/426-DISK
The Public Software Library	800/242-4775
Software Excitement	503/826-8083
The Software Labs	800/359-9998

Edit
Tip
Quote

Ignorance doesn't kill you, but it makes you sweat a lot.
—Haitian Proverb

Electronic Service Networks ("Access Providers")

Bulletin board systems are not the only choice for online or electronic access. There are several larger services, frequently referred to as *access providers*, that offer worldwide access often with just a local phone call. Although they are not called BBSs, they are really just big electronic networks, like a series of bulletin boards all connected together.

There are several differences immediately noticed between access providers and BBSs. First, access providers monitor each file for viruses, on a regular basis. This may help you feel better about receiving software from a public source. Second, remember all those topics that we said were available on different bulletin boards? Many of the larger access providers offer hundreds of different areas of interest on the same system. These areas are often called *special interest groups*, or *SIGs*. Some BBSs have these too, but not nearly on as large a scale.

Most of these larger online services are tied into local telephone access systems. This means that you can call a local phone number (not long distance!) and get into the service. This reduces one of the major costs involved with BBS access.

Be sure you're right—then go ahead.
—Davy Crockett

Like many of the larger and more popular BBSs, the online services are not free! There is sometimes a startup fee, but almost always you are charged by the minute for the amount of time you are on the system. CompuServe lets you read mail and general news at no charge above the monthly fee, but charges extra when you get into the special interest groups, or want to mail larger messages. As with the BBSs, call the services and look around a bit before making a decision that will cost you any money.

Some of the more popular systems include CompuServe, America Online, GEnie, Delphi, and Prodigy (a joint venture between IBM and Sears). Each of these provides download areas that are monitored for viruses, and offers special forums for programmers. (CompuServe has been around the longest and provides great resources for programmers.) Most of these services even have Windows-based software that is specifically designed to access their systems. Enter your name and password once, and you'll be working online as easily as you work in any other Windows program; this is certainly a quick way to get started with a new and exciting technology!

America Online	800/227-6364
CompuServe	800/848-8199
Delphi	800/695-4005
GEnie	800/638-9636
Prodigy	800/776-3449

The Internet is a global network of networks; there is no single connection to get into the Internet. There are millions of people exchanging information on the Internet each day. By paying an access provider a monthly fee, or establishing a "node" (a permanent connection set up under your own name) on the Internet, you have free access to electronic mail, discussion groups, and programs to download. The Internet offers an excellent place to go for quick answers to difficult programming problems. If you are interested in the Internet, be sure to look at the WinMail program in Chapter 6.

What's in this Book and CD-ROM for Me?

In spite of the fact that you now have several places to search for new software, let's start your journey right at home, with the CD-ROM enclosed with this book. There are several major types of software discussed here, and the software on the disk follows a similar layout. Here's what you have waiting for you.

Programmer's Assistants

Chapter 2 covers those special programs that you get attached to in your daily work. They don't necessarily have anything to do with programming, but they make the nonprogramming activities simpler. Naturally, this leaves you more time to program, and also keeps you from dropping out to DOS every time you want to do something for which you thought there was no associated Windows program. This includes discussion of some text editors, file viewers, font handling utilities, file finders, file comparison utilities, programs to kill other programs and to exit quickly from Windows, applications that play audio CDs for you (if you can pull this CD-ROM out long enough), personal information managers, address books, label generation software for your hundreds of diskettes, and more.

Language-Free and Language-Specific

Chapter 3 discusses programs and utilities for programming. Some of them are language independent: a disassembler, or tools for installing and uninstalling your own applications. Others are specific to a language or environment; support for C and C++, as well as Visual Basic and Borland Pascal with Objects, is provided by many different programs and libraries, several of which are covered in this chapter.

Glass Houses

The three most dangerous things in the world are a programmer with a soldering iron, a hardware-type with a program patch, and a user with an idea.

—*Rick Cook*

Chapter 4 covers software that is available as source code. Naturally, this makes the code quite language specific, but remember that in Windows, if you can make a piece of code into a Dynamic Link Library (DLL), you can use it from nearly any language. So the source you find here might be more useful than you might think.

Programmer's Day Off

After the many hours of programming that you endure each day, there are times when you need to have a little fun with Windows. Plus, after seeing your own application crash thirty times in the last few hours, it can be satisfying to simply see *something* run correctly! Turn to Chapter 5 when you want to take a much deserved break.

In this chapter, you'll learn about some games that are available for Windows, as well as other programs that will make your daily use of Windows more interesting. You can try some of the background pictures, screen clearing programs, sounds, and other diversions for your mind. Or, just have some fun exploring what's in this section of the book/CD-ROM.

Business Manager

Chapter 6 presents programs that perform some of the mundane business chores that take away from your profitable time. This includes time tracking and billing, invoicing, and other tasks that you'd like to delegate, but don't have a spare person to delegate them to.

there is also a discussion about a Windows-based bulletin board system. It relates to business, since there are many business uses for BBS computers (support, order taking, distribution, etc.); however, it could also be considered as a "Day Off" item for Chapter 5, or even a "Programmer's Assistant" item for Chapter 2. I guess it depends on how much time you can spend and what you want to do with a BBS. Just having a BBS to receive messages from users or salesmen is often a great time and interruption saver!

Document Library

Chapter 7 covers a good sized selection of documentation files culled from many places. These include listings from several printed programming magazines, online magazines designed specifically for electronic distribution, Windows Help files with information to share, and more. These do not generally include any programs, but include information that you can use to better yourself, your work, or your life (well, at least there are some good programming nuggets).

Pop Quiz! Or, What Else Is New?

Chapter 8 is a special test for you. In it, you are given the opportunity to hunt through a bunch of listings, kinda like you'd do if you were online with a BBS. In this chapter, you'll be able to look through some of the very latest shareware treasures, many of which were too new to even make it into the first seven chapters.

Hacking Ahead

We've talked enough about what this book holds in store for you. Turn the page, and let's get started!

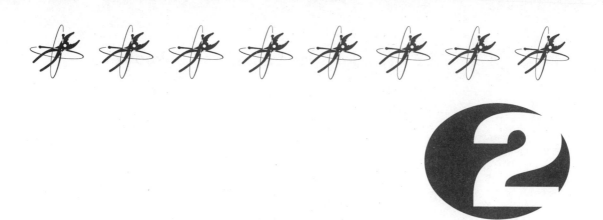

Programmer's Assistants

I remember when I started programming on the PC. Actually, I remember two different times I started programming on the PC. In early 1983, when the PC first hit the market, I worked on a small project in college, writing a gradebook "application" in BASIC. What a deal: the compiler came with the computer, as did the manual. What a change from the mainframes, where everything seemed to be an "extra."

Then I started programming for real with Turbo Pascal. I was amazed at what could be purchased for only $49—a disk and a manual, allowing development of some great programs. I could fit the compiler on my 10MB hard drive, with room to spare. The disk wasn't even compressed. And the manual had everything in it—no need to look for other information.

I used to run a 286-10 MHz, with a full megabyte of memory. Now, I'm finding that my 486-33 MHz with 20MB of memory is not quite up to the task. Recently, I installed the newest version of a Borland compiler I use. This time, I loaded it from a CD-ROM disc (rather than a dozen or so 1.4MB floppies), decompressing it onto 80MB or so of my hard drive, and this didn't even install the online documentation! The printed manuals weigh nearly as much as my four-year-old daughter. This must be progress.

You may ask, What does all this have to do with good shareware?

*Anyone who can
master a telephone
can certainly
program.*
—Bob Frankston

Well, the more complex that software development environments become, the less time programmers have free to go looking for other tools they may need. I'd like to introduce you to some of the great tools I've found in the shareware channels, all of which are included on the CD-ROM in this book. Think about it—if you are going to be stuck doing Windows programming all day, why not take advantage of anything that can make your nonprogramming activities simpler? These are the tools to help you with those tasks.

Music Is a Most Important Concept

I struggled to decide which CD player to show you, and whether the CD player should be included here or in "Programmer's Day Off" (Chapter 5). But if you're like a lot of programmers I know, the sound of music is often required for programming. Here are two to choose from, to make your work more productive, of course.

CD Wizzard (shown in Figure 2-1) is a wonderful example of a small program that's indispensible once you're used to it. Use the Wizzard to play audio CDs in your computer's CD-ROM drive. It has a nice appearance, kinda like a CD player that is part of a home stereo system. It shows the time into a song, or the time remaining on the song (your choice). The display also shows the number of songs, which song is playing, and which songs have already played. The current song number is shown in red, the ones that have played are yellow, and the ones yet to come are in green.

In addition, you can press a button and automatically have CD Wizzard repeat the track, or the entire CD. This keeps you from having to restart the CD every 52 minutes or so. If you want, you can also program the order that the songs will play in. That way, you can skip those less-enjoyable songs without having to press the Forward button every time the song starts.

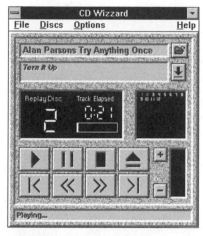

Figure 2-1. *CD Wizzard looks similar to your home stereo CD player*

Two other options allow you to let CD Wizzard pick the order the songs play in ("shuffle", they call it), or, using the Timed play mode, you can select a total amount of time you want the CD to play. This is handy to use as an alarm; when the music stops, the party's over. And, if you enter a name for each disc you put into the drive, CD Wizzard will display the name each time you reuse the disc.

```
Hack Facts

CD Player
1.1
Charles Cranford
TARDIS DP Consultants
Department 45
6 Sedley Ct.
Greensboro, NC 27455
$8
Shareware
130K
CDPLY.EXE
```

Although there are other CD players available, I choose this one, called CD Player, to also include on this CD-ROM. Why? CD Player looks less like your home stereo CD player, but it's much simpler to read.

CD Player provides many of the same features as CD Wizzard, lacking only the Timed play mode. CD Player turns the CD off when you exit, which can be handy unless you're not expecting it. CD Wizzard also has this option, so you can decide whether the disc is shut down during the exit, or whether it continues to play.

I guess there are reasons for each of the programs. One of the more basic

Don't try listening to a CD-ROM disc, rather than a CD audio disc. It doesn't work!

reasons to consider is the amount of free disk space and cash you have. CD Wizzard costs twice as much as CD Player, and takes twice the disk space, but provides more functionality. Is that worth the extra couple of bucks to you? (Remember, you've already paid for the drive!) You're talking about sacrificing the cost of a lunch or two, not that you have much time for lunching out anyway, just to give you the same feel of your home stereo. Think about it, try them both, and buy the one that better suits you.

Keeping Track of the Details

Now that you've got a CD playing, you're ready to go to work. Given the life of a programmer, I imagine that there are probably dozens (at least) of things that need to be done at once. Besides the normal six programs you're working on, there are birthdays to get cards for, prospects you want to call, dental appointments that are a year overdue, and a car that needs an inspection.

Of course, I'm sure that you have all of this written down—somewhere, right? I've always struggled with writing everything on a pad (or several), and then never being able to find it again. Why can't I keep all of it on the computer? After all, that's one of the things computers do best: keeping track of information.

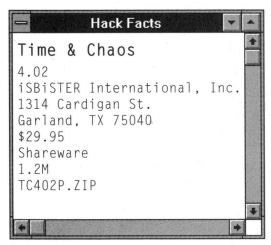

```
─  |           Hack Facts           | ▼ ▲
                                        ▲
Time & Chaos
4.02
iSBiSTER International, Inc.
1314 Cardigan St.
Garland, TX 75040
$29.95
Shareware
1.2M
TC402P.ZIP
                                        ▼
  ◄ |                              | ►
```

Two excellent programs exist in Windows shareware to help solve this problem. The first is my personal favorite for a quick, easy-to-learn, but capable program. I think the real reason I initially liked it is because of its name, Time & Chaos. This is representative of not only my desk and my office, but of my mind in general.

Time & Chaos (shown in Figure 2-2) is designed to keep your appointments, phone book, and lists of things that really ought to be done. And, since we don't yet have a law making carrying a portable computer mandatory for each citizen, there's a nice printing feature to produce paper versions of the information to keep with you.

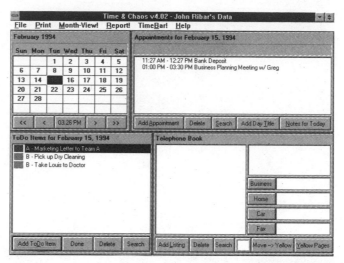

Figure 2-2. *Time & Chaos is simple to understand and use*

*You can't do just
one thing.*
*—Campbell's Law of
Everything*

The layout of Time & Chaos is very simple, showing your appointments, To-Do list, and phone book from the main screen. There are some very useful features built-in. For instance, when you add something to the To-Do list, you can link it to a phone book entry. Then, when you try to do the thing that needs to be done, the phone number is handy (try doing that with your pad of paper system!). When you add items to your appointment list, you can have them automatically scheduled on the basis of the following time periods: daily, weekly, monthly, yearly, on the same day each month, on the same day every other week, or every so many days. Now you won't forget all those appointments that recur yet are too easily forgotten until the last minute.

Time & Chaos will dial the phone for you, assuming, of course, that you have a modem connected to an appropriate port on your computer. Four phone numbers can be maintained for each person, including home, work, car phone, and fax.

when you want to edit any of the items on the main screen, you are taken to specialized views of the information. This gives you a little more room to work. If you are trying to schedule appointments, the weekly and monthly views are great. But an even more exciting tool, at least in our office, is the TimeBar feature. This screen shows all of your time allocation for the current month, in a spreadsheet-like manner. Across the top are the days, and down the side are the hours. This in itself is nice for determining open time for scheduling meetings, appointments, etc. But what is even more useful is the ability to superimpose the schedule of someone else on the network! This way, you can quickly schedule group meetings, knowing that the time selected is not a burden for anyone involved.

If you don't need *major* scheduling features, and just want to keep track of some information you use on a daily basis, Time & Chaos is a great package. If, however, you require something like the more robust scheduling capabilities of the major time management programs, you might look instead at Above & Beyond.

Above & Beyond is a little more expensive, takes more disk space, and takes a little longer to learn than Time & Chaos. But the resulting efficiency can be a great boost. Again, this is a better package if you have some training in time management, have a little more time to spend maintaining your information, and don't mind the additional monetary and disk space requirements.

Above & Beyond has functions that are similar to Time & Chaos, but they are handled in a different manner. There is a feature for those of you that must carry a computer everywhere, so that you can keep your desktop and laptop computers synchronized. This is extremely useful, especially if you have ever tried doing this manually!

There are also special features for scheduling network users. A manager can watch the schedules and work loads of everyone on the network without having to call and bother each of them. In addition, group scheduling becomes a snap. Messages can be sent to arrange meetings or just pass along telephone calls.

In either of these programs, if you want to work as a workgroup, be sure to budget some time each day for updating your schedules. Maybe you'll even need several times (of shorter duration) per day. If this time is not used, there might be little gain in productivity; scheduling meetings and planning work loads based on outdated information is extremely dangerous, especially if it's you that gets the extra work!

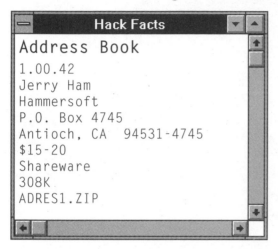

Not everyone will want to keep track of everything. In fact, very often all that's needed is a simple program dedicated to tracking names and addresses. Address Book (shown in Figure 2-3) is just one of these programs. It's smaller than the information managers like Time & Chaos and Above & Beyond, but still fills a void in Windows' capabilities.

Address Book looks very simple when it starts up, just like a list of people with phone numbers. Amazing, isn't it? If you add a name, or double-click on one to edit it, you're greeted with a larger screen, which holds the person's phone, fax, and modem numbers. It also includes their address, a secondary address, birthdate, anniversary date, and a space for free-form notes.

One plus for Address Book is that it prints very nice looking rolodex cards for all or selected people in your phone book. It can also print mailing labels. If you don't need the power of a personal information manager (PIM), something like Address Book would be a wise choice for maintaining your name and address lists.

Stuff Related to Programming

Now that you have the music playing, and have decided what it is you're supposed to do for the day, you might get to begin programming. Well, maybe *get to* isn't the right phrase. It's time to start programming, like it or not. So here are some tools to help you along.

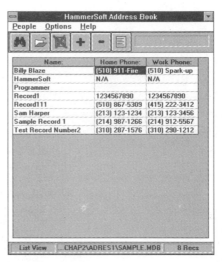

Figure 2-3. *Address Book fills the void for a small, dedicated address book*

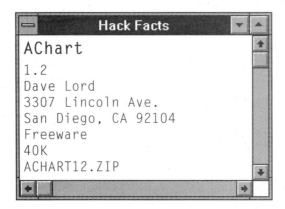

AChart, shown in Figure 2-4, is a great little tool that replaces all those charts you have tacked on the wall. It's an ASCII chart, but not just a simple chart of all the characters, as you might expect.

AChart includes a display of the ANSI chart (using all the serial transmission character designations), a version with control characters (^A, ^B, ^C, etc.), and a third version with the IBM PC character set (including all the line drawing characters).

Along with that, AChart has a display of the EBCDIC characters, and even a display of the current palette (showing the colors in use for the current program). Throw away your appendices from those old programming manuals; here is the only program you'll need for finding this valuable information.

It's too bad this wasn't available when everyone was doing a lot of DOS programming. Under Windows, the PC line drawing characters aren't used too much, and who ever

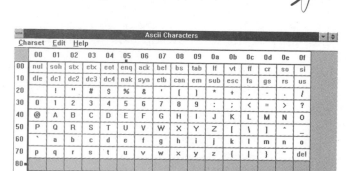

Figure 2-4.   *AChart shows everything you'll need to know about ASCII characters (and ANSI, EBCDIC, and IBM PC)*

heard of EBCDIC anyway? But seriously, this is a great tool for lots of reasons.

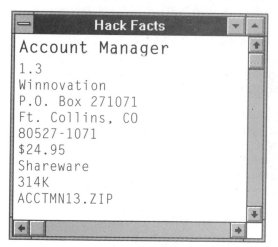

Hack Facts

Account Manager

1.3
Winnovation
P.O. Box 271071
Ft. Collins, CO
80527-1071
$24.95
Shareware
314K
ACCTMN13.ZIP

If you're like many programmers, you need to keep track of the work that you do in order to receive a paycheck. Two programs that can help you with this task are Account Manager and TaskTracker. Both programs allow you to track time against a specific project, which, in my opinion, is a requirement for this type of program. And of course, reports are available to show where you spent your time. I decided to include both programs because of the differences in how they handle time tracking.

Account Manager has a unique approach. If you so desire, Account Manager can automatically make entries in your time-tracking database each time you enter or exit a Windows application. For instance, if you're working on a project, you can now track the amount of time you are in the compiler environment (programming, we assume), in the word processor (writing documentation), in the drawing package of choice (drawing pictures for late birthday cards, or perhaps for the manual), or in the games you play to relax your mind. If much of the work you do is tracked in this way, this system is ideal.

Luckily, you don't have to track every program you use. You specifically designate which programs are of interest, and what project you want the time billed against. You can also designate that you log in when one application starts, but log out when another one starts (or finishes). You can also log in and out without being tied to a specific Windows application. The possibilities are endless!

Account Manager also comes with a DOS program that allows you to check in and out even if you are outside of Windows. But, why would you ever be out of Windows?

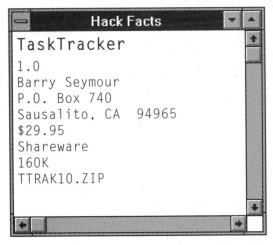

```
┌─────────────────────────────────────┐
│ ─  ▼        Hack Facts        ▼  ▲  │
├─────────────────────────────────┬───┤
│ TaskTracker                     │ ▲ │
│                                 ├───┤
│ 1.0                             │   │
│ Barry Seymour                   │   │
│ P.O. Box 740                    │   │
│ Sausalito, CA  94965            │   │
│ $29.95                          │   │
│ Shareware                       │   │
│ 160K                            │   │
│ TTRAK10.ZIP                     │   │
│                                 ├───┤
│                                 │ ▼ │
├───┬─────────────────────────┬───┼───┤
│ ◀ │                         │ ▶ │   │
└───┴─────────────────────────┴───┴───┘
```

TaskTracker is different. In this program, shown in Figure 2-5, you simply check in and out, applying your time against a specific project. There is no relationship with the actual programs that you run. TaskTracker shows the current amount of time incurred below its icon. This is handy when you are billed by the hour, and want to know if you are spending too much time on a specific task.

When you're finished with a billing period, and have sent an invoice for your time (or just prepared a report for your client), you can then generate a new copy of the project worksheet, with all the times automatically reset to zero. No need to clear the totals manually; you can start the new time period fresh with minimal effort.

The only thing I haven't figured out is why the TaskTracker icon always says 01:23. This isn't the elapsed time; that's shown separately. The icon just says 01:23. Just remember to look in the right place for your data.

These are two great packages for tracking time spent on projects. Reminiscent of our discussion about time

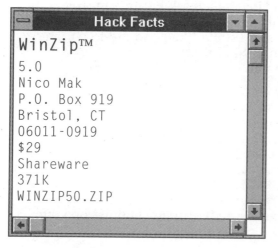

Figure 2-5. *TaskTracker has a simple-to-understand demeanor*

managers early in this chapter, one of these programs is simpler to learn and use (TaskTracker), while the other is more robust, providing additional capabilities for those that need them (Account Manager).

Managing Your Hard Drives

Much of the shareware you get from any source will be in a compressed format. This is done to save the number of disks required for distribution, and to reduce the amount of time you must spend on long-distance phone calls downloading the newest versions.

```
Hack Facts
WinZip™
5.0
Nico Mak
P.O. Box 919
Bristol, CT
06011-0919
$29
Shareware
371K
WINZIP50.ZIP
```

There are several major types of compression formats available for "archiving" files, and you can tell which one has been used by looking at the file extension. The most popular archive extensions include ZIP, ARC, LZH, and ARJ. The programs used to create, maintain, and extract from these archives are mostly DOS-based. Their names are similar to the related file extensions: PKZIP and PKUNZIP (ZIP files), ARJ (ARJ files), ARC (and others, for ARC files), and LHA (LZH files).

But from Windows, it's a real problem to keep dropping out to DOS just to see

Create a directory for your extraction before running WinZip. Or let WinZip create it for you!

what's in an archive file. WinZip, shown in Figure 2-6, is a tool that removes this drudgery, allowing quick access to your archive files from within Windows. Select an archive file and WinZip shows its contents.

Then, by simply pushing the correct button, you can add to or extract from the archive. In addition, WinZip has a special feature called CheckOut. In this mode, a Program Manager group is created for the archive, and an icon is created for each file in the archive. What a great way to checkout what's in an archive!

WinZip also supports using a virus scanner on your archives, and can create self-extracting EXE files from your archives. All in all, this is one of the best utilities to add to your Windows repertoire.

Another tool that's well-versed in file management is Command Post. This program has so many features that I'm bound not to mention them all. In a nutshell, Command Post is a replacement for the Windows File Manager, and even handles most of the work normally delegated to the Program Manager and Task Manager.

Command Post, shown in Figure 2-7, uses text-based file lists, rather than the graphics-based information shown in File Manager. What this means is that the screen updates are much, much faster (kinda like good old DOS). The only thing that you lose, as far as I have found, is the drag-and-drop capabilites of File Manager.

There are enough other reasons to switch to Command Post, however. All the file associations you set up in File Manager still work, so TXT files are handled through the Notepad, DOC files by Word for Windows, HLP files by the Windows Help system, and ZIP files are handled through WinZip (if you liked what you read earlier).You can format a floppy, check the amount of space remaining on a floppy, log into and out of the network, check system resources, add and extract files from a ZIP archive file, rearrange the active, open Windows on your desktop (in one of several orientations), switch to other

Name	Date	Time	Size	Ratio	Packed	Path
cdplayer.exe	08/18/92	01:00	106,732	58%	45,486	
cdplayer.hlp	08/18/92	01:00	58,151	25%	44,145	
readme.txt	08/18/92	01:00	5,653	54%	2,625	
setup.exe	07/11/92	17:31	13,888	43%	7,953	
setup.lst	08/02/92	13:34	14	0%	14	
setup1.exe	08/18/92	01:00	29,576	53%	13,996	
setupkit.dl_	07/11/92	17:31	7,008	58%	2,991	
vbrun100.dl_	05/10/91	01:00	271,264	38%	169,067	
ver.dl_	07/11/92	17:31	8,736	40%	5,293	
mci.vbx	07/11/92	17:31	36,944	60%	14,844	
picclip.vbx	07/11/92	17:31	12,944	50%	6,601	

Figure 2-6. *Just selecting an archive file immediately shows its contents. Adding to or extracting from files is just as simple*

active tasks (like Task Manager does), change the wallpaper, or even start the screen blanker immediately.

Read the docs. They're often as fun as the programs.

That's all it can do, right? Nope, there's lots more. Have you ever had the desire to work with entire directories at one time? Command Post will allow you to copy, move, or even delete an entire directory structure. Don't worry, before you can delete an entire directory structure, you're given three tries to change your mind. The questions are well thought out and insightful:

1. "You are about to delete all kinds of stuff containing possibly 10 zillion files and subdirs. Continue?"

2. "Shall we stop now and not delete anything?" (Notice that this one requires the opposite answer, making you think even more about what you're doing.)

3. "CONTINUE???!!!??? Are you sure you can find your backups???"

If you finally give up after the third try, you're given the message, "Well then, we better not play around with nuclear devices." Is any of this necessary? No. I'm sure the program would work the same with three plain old "Are You Sure?"

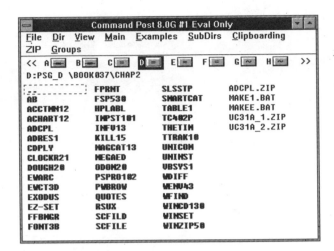

Figure 2-7. *Command Post sports a quick, easy-to-read textual interface.*

messages, but what fun is that? I know I have enough things in my briefcase that are repetitive and less than fun. It's nice to see programs with some personality of their own. As long as they allow me to make the final decision, of course.

Command Post also includes a feature for finding files. But if you really want a file finder, WFind, described next, is an excellent addition to your Windows program stack.

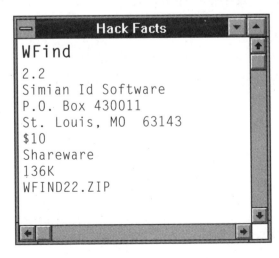

Do you ever put things away in just the right place so you'll be able to find them again? Why is it then you can never find them later? This happens to me on the computer sometimes. You may be perfectly organized and can always remember where your files are located. Me? I *know* I copied those backup files somewhere but, um...I can't find them just now.

WFind is a program designed not only to find files for which you know the name, but also to find files that contain a few letters you remember, or files whose names match a regular expression that you specify.

For instance, you can easily search for all *.BAK files using most file search programs. But suppose you want to find all the accounting files for 1994 that were from the southeastern district? If the files had names like SEMay94.DAT, SEJune94.DAT, etc., you couldn't do the search with most programs. (DOS * wildcards don't allow any text after the *. So the best you could hope for is all the files starting with SE*, for all years. Of course, if you knew there were always three letters, you could use SE???94.DAT. But June is four letters, and May is three; WFind is easier, trust me!) Using a regular expression in WFind, you can look for filenames that start with SE and end with 94. Simply and easily.

What's So Regular About It?

A regular expression is something that's used in pattern matching. Why it's called regular, I'm not sure. It's a sequence of characters that "means match these characters," "match any characters not in this set," "match this character at the beginning of a word," etc. I can't teach it all to you here, but the documentation for WFind will help you out. If you've ever used GREP (generalized regular expression parser) to find information in a file, you may have had experience with regular expressions already.

WFind also gives you another option. You could ask for a list of all files that start with SE and were created between the dates 1/1/94 and 12/31/94. The capability to look for date and time stamps in your search, as well as file sizes, is a unique addition.

Think how easy it'll now be to find those leftover Windows application temp files. Simply look for all files that start with the tilde (~), and have a date before today. Those space hogs can now be deleted in a flash!

Tracking What Windows Is Doing

What happens when you didn't really want to run that hot deletion utility you just wrote and now all of your Windows directories are being consumed?

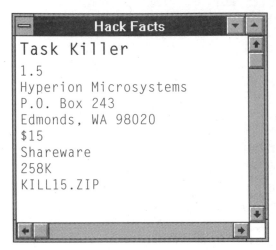

Hack Facts

Task Killer
1.5
Hyperion Microsystems
P.O. Box 243
Edmonds, WA 98020
$15
Shareware
258K
KILL15.ZIP

Admit it. Sometimes your programs don't work right the first time. Or they get themselves stuck in infinite loops. Or the report that's being generated won't quite fit on your hard disk. It happens to us all. So, how do you stop these runaways?

It's simple, if you use Task Killer. But Task Killer, shown in Figure 2-8, is an exciting utility for many other reasons. Task Killer, which uses a subtle Tyrannosaurus Rex head as its icon, shows you a lot of information about the tasks that are currently running under Windows, even if you don't want to kill any of them.

Tip

Don't kill tasks unless you're sure what they're for, or you might hang the whole system!

You can see all the EXE programs running, all the DLL files that are loaded, the fonts and drivers that are loaded, and even the VBX files in use (for all those new Visual Basic programs). You see the source of each file (where the original file is located on the disk), the file size in memory, and the number of times the task is running, or DLL is in use.

Using the extended display will even show you the version information for each of the files. Now you can see the date and time the DLL was created (this is especially nice when you have to call for support). If you are really checking out what's going on in your system, you can even display the common modules used throughout Windows: Display, Kernel, GDI, System, Comm, User, Keyboard, Mouse, and Sound.

There are lots of things you can do with this display. You can have several displays at once (one of just EXEs, one with DLLs, another with VBXs), and watch how they change as your newest program runs. There's also an option to print

Name	Usage	Size	Date/Time	
DISPLAY	37	73200	03/10/92	03:10 AM	c
FRES	1	13472	03/22/93	02:00 AM	d
KILLER	1	206800	01/26/94	09:07 PM	d
LZEXPAND	1	23712	11/01/93	03:11 AM	c
MMSYSTEM	11	61648	11/01/93	03:11 AM	c
NDDEAPI	2	16096	11/01/93	03:11 AM	c
NDDENB	1	15136	11/01/93	03:11 AM	c
NETAPI	4	108464	11/01/93	03:11 AM	c

For Help, press F1   NUM

Figure 2-8.   *Task Killer doesn't just kill programs. It shows a great deal of valuable information about all the tasks active under Windows*

Results! Why, man, I have gotten a lot of results. I know seven thousand things that won't work.
—Thomas Edison

the lists, so you can document to your boss that you really aren't the only one using the Microsoft Common Dialog DLL (the printout will show how many times each DLL is in use. If the number is greater than 1, you're not alone!).

Of course, the original purpose behind Task Killer was to stop a rampant process. This is simply done by pointing to the process, DLL, etc., and then telling it to go away (with an appropriate menu selection).

The real thing you have to watch here is what might happen if you kill a DLL that is loaded, and in use by another process. Some applications may be smart enough to reload the DLL, but you may not want to take your chances. Put on your "Super-duper wizard-level watch-what-you're-doing-you-could-hurt-someone" thinking cap before you start killing shared files! And if you're on a network, don't forget what it was like last time it crashed and all 47 people called you to ask why they couldn't get at the work they had done for the last three hours. (Did they save their work on a regular basis? Nooo, but when the system goes down, you're not in a position to ask!)

```
─        Hack Facts        ▼ ▲
PWBrowse                        ▲
1.0
WINDOWS Magazine
600 Community Dr.
Manhasset, NY  11030
Freeware
105K
PWBROW.ZIP                      ▼
◄                              ►
```

Another program that's useful in support situations is PWBrowse. This program displays the information found in the header of Windows applications and DLLs. While not all programs include all of this information, some of the data is almost always available.

Why do you want this information, anyway? Well, suppose that you're writing a really big document. Not the kind that the software companies call big; they usually refer to large document handling features as dealing with as many as 25 pages in a document. I'm talking about a *really* big document, I guess, say around 200 pages. As you're working, the program decides that it can no longer save the file for you. You quickly jump to the File Manager, and try to wipe out any files that you can. Nope, no better.

SO you call the support line for what was, up until now, your favorite word processor. Once you get through, a few days later, having left your machine running day and night so you won't lose the file and all the work you did, the first thing they ask for is the version of the program you're running. Do you try getting the information from the program itself, causing a crash? No, you whip out PWBrowse, shown in Figure 2-9, and read to them from the resulting screen. Now they can explain to you what the problem is (and how it was corrected in the next version released right after the one you purchased), and why there was no reason to leave your machine idle all this time (you'll have to type it all in while you wait for the update).

Hopefully, your next catastrophe that begs for support won't be so drastic. But it happens (that's a true story), so it's good to be prepared.

Another good use for PWBrowse is to check the versions of all the DLL and VBX files that are arriving with new software.

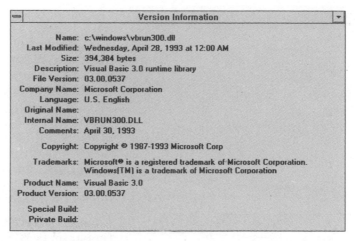

Version Information
Name: c:\windows\vbrun300.dll
Last Modified: Wednesday, April 28, 1993 at 12:00 AM
Size: 394,384 bytes
Description: Visual Basic 3.0 runtime library
File Version: 03.00.0537
Company Name: Microsoft Corporation
Language: U.S. English
Original Name:
Internal Name: VBRUN300.DLL
Comments: April 30, 1993
Copyright: Copyright © 1987-1993 Microsoft Corp
Trademarks: Microsoft® is a registered trademark of Microsoft Corporation. Windows(TM) is a trademark of Microsoft Corporation
Product Name: Visual Basic 3.0
Product Version: 03.00.0537
Special Build:
Private Build:

Figure 2-9. *PWBrowse shows you all the pertinent information about the Windows executables and support files on your system. Too bad this information is optional; not everyone supplies it with their programs*

You really only need a single copy of these files, so if the versions are all the same, get rid of some of them (how many copies of VBRUN*.DLL do you have?). Use WFind (discussed earlier in the chapter) to locate the duplicates, PWBrowse to check the version information, and Command Post (also discussed earlier) to delete the copies. Boy, you're really on your way to becoming a shareware guru now!

one final thing about PWBrowse is worth mentioning. PWBrowse was originally presented in the December 1993 and January 1994 issues of *WINDOWS* Magazine. It includes all the source code and files required to rebuild it. This means that you have documentation and the ability to add any other functions to PWBrowse that you desire. Not bad for free! By the way, the program is referred to as VER in the magazine.

I remember way back in the dinosaur days when the only way to find the differences between two files was by using the old ocular muscles (eyes, that is). Then, programs came about that would list the differences on the screen, scrolling past faster than a speeding bullet. Many of these "diff" utilities didn't do a very good job with insertions either; if you added a paragraph to a document, they would never match again, even though three lines down they should be the same.

A modern day tool for checking revisions is WDiff, a Windows application that displays the differences between two versions of a text file, side by side. This is a long way from the original diff utilities.

WDiff, shown in Figure 2-10, is handy for checking revisions of source code, and therefore seems to be a great programming tool. But it's also good for more run-of-the-mill tasks. For instance, each time you install a new program or application, your AUTOEXEC.BAT, CONFIG.SYS, and WIN.INI

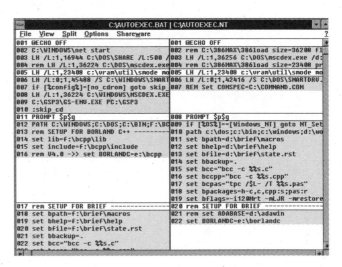

Figure 2-10.   *WDiff shows you the differences in text files, side by side*

Edit
Tip
Quote

That must be wonderful; I have no idea what it means.
—Moliere

files (as well as others) may get changed. How would you know what was altered?

If you have to go through your files manually, this can be a tedious task. Using WDiff, you simply compare the AUTOEXEC.OLD file (usually created by the setup or installation program) with the new AUTOEXEC.BAT file. Voilà! There are the differences! Now you can decide whether to let them ride, or change them back.

WDiff presents an excellent display of the file differences. The two files are shown next to each other, with the changes highlighted. When the files match again, they are matched side by side in the display. This makes for a very effective determination of where changes are located. WDiff gives you the option of whether to show the unchanged portions. If you disable this option, it's more difficult to locate the changes in the actual file, but you get a quick overview of what has actually been altered.

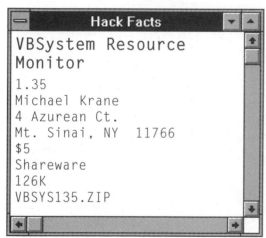

Hack Facts

VBSystem Resource Monitor
1.35
Michael Krane
4 Azurean Ct.
Mt. Sinai, NY   11766
$5
Shareware
126K
VBSYS135.ZIP

Another tool that allows you to check what Windows is doing, and in fact how your whole system is doing, is VBSystem Resource Monitor. This resource monitoring package, shown in Figure 2-11, sits unobtrusively on your screen and displays all the information you probably need to know about what your system is doing.

On a periodic basis (any update period you select), VBSystem shows the number of tasks running and the amount of system resources still available. You also get to watch the disk drives fill up, and the amount of memory that remains as all your applications run.

This is a nifty little utility that performs the functions of several other programs. For instance, since the time and date are shown, there's no reason to run Clock. There is a quick Exit feature, called by pressing the program's X button. If you so choose, Windows will immediately exit, without a question to you first. All of your applications are closed correctly, but you don't need to answer Yes to a question you thought was self-explanatory ("Yes, I asked you to exit

Figure 2-11. *VBSystem shows you how your system is doing, including displaying the time and the date. Very useful for those all-night programming sessions*

VBSystem will let you exit without any confirmation!

because I really wanted to exit"). Guess what? There's also a Restart Windows button, so you can restart without dropping all the way out to DOS first. This is really handy when you have an application that goes south, and Windows tells you to restart. Let's hope you don't experience this too often, but at least the capability to recover is there.

You can tell VBSystem to always remain on top of the active window. This is helpful in program testing situations, where you want to know the impact that your new application will have on your system.

There is an extended information screen, called by pressing the program's M button (for More information). It shows the processor and coprocessor you're using, versions of the system software (DOS and Windows), which video driver and resolution you're using, the amount of several resources that are available, and much more. Overall, this is a great utility to keep in the corner of your screen.

Keeping Track of Floppies

In the course of developing new software, regularly backing up the work you're doing, or beginning to work with shareware, filling hundreds of floppies with all sorts of things, you'll want to start labeling some of those disks. Otherwise, how will you ever find anything?

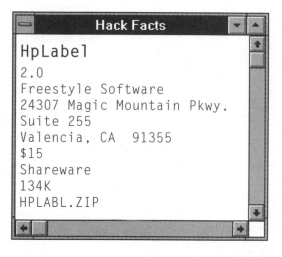

HpLabel, shown in Figure 2-12, is just the ticket if you have a Hewlett-Packard laser or deskjet printer, or something that's compatible. HpLabel allows you to print labels for 5¼" or 3½" floppies, using the precut labels from Avery (and other suppliers).

Start HpLabel, and you're presented with a diagram of the sheet of labels to be printed. Select a label with the mouse. Now you can add a title to the label, specific to your disk (Project 1 Backup, CIS Downloads from 10/15, etc.). This isn't labeling the disk itself, it's just printing a title on the label.

Now for the really hard part. Put the floppy into the drive. That's all! HpLabel reads the files and formats them for printing on the label you selected. Next, select another label and continue the process.

This sounds too easy, doesn't it? No handwriting labels, no errors or omissions, everything is legible. And if you have

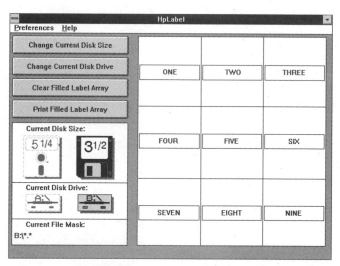

Figure 2-12. *Pick a label, any label, and HpLabel will fill it with information about your floppy disk. You can even give it a name*

unenlightened friends who don't do Windows, there are even non-Windows versions available. The only drawback is buying the special labels, and feeding them through the laser printer correctly on the first try. Believe me, after wasting a few of these labels, you get good really fast!

Hack Facts

SmartCat Plus

1.10
Shareable Software
 International, Inc.
P.O. Box 59102
Schaumburg, IL 60159
$39.95
Shareware
644K
SMARTCAT.ZIP

Of course, just putting labels on diskettes doesn't make things totally easy to find. Reading the labels on 400 disks still takes a lot of time. Look into SmartCat Plus, a disk cataloging program. I was going to say a disk*ette* cataloging program, but SmartCat Plus is also excellent for tracking the files on you new CD-ROMs.

You simply tell SmartCat Plus to read a disk, and the files are placed into the database. SmartCat Plus reads archive files, too, so you can find an old letter stored in an outdated archive as easily as the latest version of VBRUN300.DLL.

As you place each disk into SmartCat Plus, you're allowed to add a comment. This is useful for tracking what the types of files are. Remember how you did that with HpLabel to place a title on your labels? Using the same title as the comment here can aid in finding the disks later.

SmartCat Plus can automatically read comments from many file types, and several extensions are available to add additional file types. For instance, when reading a font file, there's an extension that creates a comment which includes the font name.

Now when you need to find a file, you have a method to determine which disk it's on. If you have your disks in some sort of order (alphabetically by disk title, for instance), it's quick and easy to find the right disk. Check the label you created with HpLabel, and if you have a match, you've found the file. If they don't match, the SmartCat Plus entry and label were not made at the same time, and it's time to try again. This won't take long, provided you can find those blasted sheets of labels again.

Working Around the Office

There are hundreds of new applications being created for the Windows environment. Many of them have at least some bearing on the things a programmer does all day. Sometimes the correlation is direct, and sometimes it's a stretch. In this section, we'll stretch a little and talk about some of the office-type applications that can be helpful, and may even be pertinent to the things you do every day.

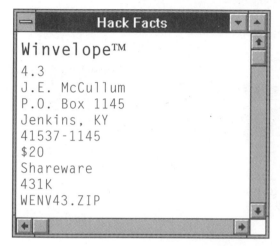

```
Hack Facts

Winvelope™
4.3
J.E. McCullum
P.O. Box 1145
Jenkins, KY
41537-1145
$20
Shareware
431K
WENV43.ZIP
```

The first thing you think about when you think "office work" is envelope addressing, right? Well, maybe not. But you'll think about it more when you look at this application. Winvelope is a fantastic package for addressing envelopes using an HP-compatible laser printer. I know, you're probably asking why addressing envelopes should be so important. Who cares, right? Wrong!

First of all, with all the time I've spent on the keyboard, my handwriting muscles are getting weaker and weaker. Sure, I can cut the number of addresses in half by using return address labels, or paying lots of money for preprinted envelopes. But what if there are several addresses I want to use, or I want to show our logo. I'd hate to hand draw it each time!

Do I have your attention yet? Let's talk about Winvelope. This package, shown in Figure 2-13, is used to print both return and mailing addresses on envelopes. You can select the size of envelope you wish to use. In fact, if you use multiple return addresses, you can select a different sized envelope for each address (number 6 for mail from home, number 10 from the office, etc.).

Yes, you can store as many return addresses as you like. Do you think one is enough? Try using different addresses with a short message on the last line ("Thanks for your business," "Your bill is overdue," "Thanks for the visit," "Our new software is terrific," etc.). Even if you only have one mailing address, you may want to use several return address layouts.

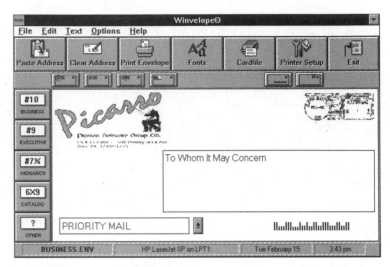

Figure 2-13. *Winvelope brings new style and class to your letter-sending chores*

About the logo I mentioned: instead of simple text, you can select a bitmap image to use as the return address. Preprinted envelopes without preprinting! This is a terrific image enhancer!

now

for the financial facts. The Postal Service now offers a discount if you use ZIP+4 codes with a Postnet barcode. Are you going to write these all by hand? Of course not. But Winvelope will print the Postnet barcode for you, if you just supply the ZIP+4 code in the address. You don't even need to mark it or retype it for this to happen. Now you have a financial incentive to use Winvelope.

How about the need to send something out to the same group of people each time (your beta testers, for instance)? Winvelope lets you pull mailing addresses from a Cardfile, or even through the Windows Copy and Paste feature. You may never have to type another address more than once again (write a letter in Word for Windows, copy the addressee information, paste into Winvelope, print the envelope, paste the address into Cardfile for future use; whew! what a time saver).

are you convinced yet? Winvelope is a great utility to have around. Even programmers send mail, and the envelopes look really nice using Winvelope. By the way, you can change the font for each of your return addresses (script or handwritten for home, sans serif or specialty font for the office, etc.).

Hack Facts

FontSpec Pro

5.3
UniTech Corporation
2697 McKelvey Rd.
Maryland Heights, MO   63043
$25
Shareware
510K
FSP530.ZIP

I mentioned that you can change the fonts for Winvelope. This can produce a professional image or just be used for the fun of it. Whatever the reason, which font you select can make all the difference. Therefore, you need to know about the two font management packages included with this book.

The first package is FontSpec Pro, one of the best and most complete font managers I've ever seen. FontSpec Pro, shown in Figure 2-14, is actually a set of several programs. First, a viewing package allows you to see what the fonts will all look like on screen. Yes, you could do this in your favorite word processor, but chances are it would be slow and cumbersome. In the

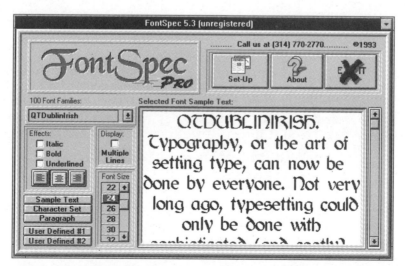

Figure 2-14.   *FontSpec Pro lets you see how fonts will look, in several different formats. Sorry, but you still have to make the final decision*

FontSpec Pro viewer, just select a font from the list of those available, and you're shown a multiline example; you can choose to see the alphabet, a short test paragraph, or a selection you type in manually. This way, you get several views of what the final output will look like. You can even select the type size and other attributes (bold, italic, underline) to see all aspects of the font in question.

Once you've made your selection, head back to your word processor and continue your work. But FontSpec Pro isn't finished. It also has the capability to manage groups of fonts. You probably know by now that Windows takes longer to load, as do many applications, if there is a large number of fonts installed. This is aggravated by programs like CorelDRAW (a fantastic package, but...) which has some 750 or more fonts.

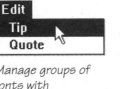

Manage groups of fonts with FontSpec Pro. It saves lots of time.

The FontSpec Pro font manager lets you select groups of fonts, and then install and uninstall them as desired, in named groups. You can create a group that has the fancy fonts you use for your newsletter, another that has the book-like fonts for your manuals and proposals, and another that has the handwriting fonts you use for personal correspondence. Of course, you'll probably want to keep a final group that has all the fonts loaded, for those especially creative periods. Installing a new group is simple. No file copying, no Control Panel Font applet. Just select the group you want, and the Font Manager does the rest.

There are two options for getting printed examples of all your fonts. FontSpec Pro has a printing utility that creates pages it calls Typeface Collection sheets. These are dual-column pages with sample text and names of each of the fonts you have installed. A very nice addition for the side of your filing cabinet, right next to the menu for the take-out Chinese restaurant down the street.

The next program is much smaller and less expensive, but you also give up some of the features of FontSpec Pro. Both are good additions, and your choice can probably be determined by how much you play around with your fonts.

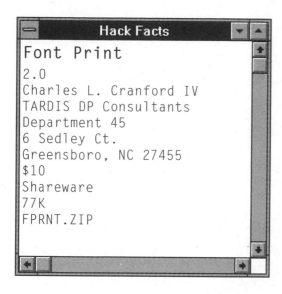

```
Hack Facts

Font Print

2.0
Charles L. Cranford IV
TARDIS DP Consultants
Department 45
6 Sedley Ct.
Greensboro, NC 27455
$10
Shareware
77K
FPRNT.ZIP
```

Font Print is another option for font printouts. Font Print doesn't come with all the bells and whistles of FontSpec Pro, but it does a very good job at its single purpose: printing font sheets.

Font Print actually prints more of an example for each font, attempting to show the entire character set. If the font is too wide, you won't see the last few letters, since only one line is used to print each example. The fonts stick out in an easy-to-read manner; printing the report in a single column allows for more example text, but creates a longer report.

Font Print is ideal if you just want to print your font list every now and then. You can print all of your fonts, or any combination. This could be nice for documentation; simply list the "approved" fonts for your manual or newsletter, and pass the list out to those who are involved. No more guessing if the font is right.

```
Hack Facts

Paint Shop Pro

2.01
JASC, Inc.
10901 Red Circle Dr.
Suite 340
Minnetonka, MN  55343
$69
Shareware
528K
PSPRO201.ZIP
```

Fonts aren't the only things that need to be managed for use in your documents and programs. Some of the greatest growth in programming, as well as in document preparation, is in the use of graphics. I recently talked with a woman who was creating a newsletter using a popular word processor, but leaving blank areas where she would later paste up pictures she cut out of a clip-art magazine.

I told her about the tens of thousands of clip-art images available online, and asked why she was planning on pasting those by hand. She gave me two

2

answers: she didn't know about the availability of online clipart, and she didn't know how to convert the artwork into the correct image file format.

Both of these are valid concerns. The first one we can't help; if you know about something you're bound to use it, and if you don't, you won't be able to (that's the reason for this book, actually). The second problem can be managed using Paint Shop Pro.

Paint Shop Pro is a graphics capture and conversion utility. It allows you to read in any of the following file types: BMP, DIB, GIF, IMG, JAS, MAC, MSP, PCX, PIC, RAS, RLE, TGA, TIF, and WPG. Once you load the image, you can resize it, change the number of colors used, and perform other manipulations.

Thinking is tiring, and may prevent other thinking
—Gerald Weinberg

You'll probably then want to save this new creation. Generate any of the following file types: BMP (Windows or OS/2), DIB (Windows or OS/2), GIF, PCX (version 2 or 5), PIC, RLE, TIF, or WPG.

This is a very handy feature by itself. But Paint Shop Pro goes much further. You can capture screen images with it, full or partial screen, to be stored and displayed within Paint Shop Pro itself. This is a quick way to grab screen images for inclusion in your documents. If you cut more than you wanted, just try again. These images can be placed on the Clipboard (to be pasted into other applications), or can be saved to a file in the formats listed above.

For many programmers, Paint Shop Pro will be the only graphics program they'll ever need. It's full of features, simple and straightforward to use, and inexpensive when compared to similar retail programs.

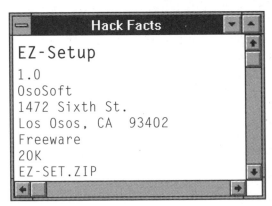

Eventually, you'll probably purchase some retail software, or you'll purchase some registered shareware.

In either case, there will be a file on the first floppy disk called SETUP or INSTALL. Most of the time, the documentation instructs you to insert the disk, select Run from the Program Manager File menu, and then type in the name (SETUP or INSTALL) of the program to be run. Sounds familiar, right?

EZ-Setup runs those diskette-based installation programs with a single click.

This is fine and dandy, but gets to be rather a nuisance if done very often. If this is always the first step, why can't it be automated? OsoSoft had the same question, and produced a free package called EZ-Setup.

EZ-Setup does only one thing. It looks on your A and B drives, searching for an INSTALL.EXE or SETUP.EXE program file. If found, the program is run. If neither of the files is found on either drive, a message tells you so.

There isn't much else to say about EZ-Setup. It's small, cheap, and works well for the single function it performs. Sometimes this is the best type of utility to find!

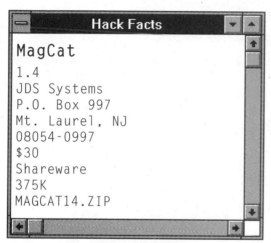

Many of these types of utilities are first presented in magazines (like PWBrowse from earlier in this chapter). If you're like me, trying to go back and find an article (or anything!) you vaguely remember reading somewhere is almost as daunting as having to sort through a basket full of floppies for one file. Well, earlier in this chapter we showed you there's a way to quickly find files by introducing you to SmartCat Plus. But now, what to do about keeping track of all those articles?

MagCat is a specialized database program, designed for maintaining article and book reference material. In the past, my system had always been to keep stacks of magazines with little tags of paper peeking out from between the pages. This is the efficient way I kept track of the interesting stuff. Funny, but I never quite figured out how to ever find it again—until MagCat, that is.

MagCat allows you to enter the article name, source, and location for each item of interest. For magazines, this includes the issue information. The location can be "Box 12 in the Attic," "Second shelf from the left," or the name of an online, scanned image file.

Three data files are maintained. First, a list of the valid locations is kept. This prevents you from having to retype the information each time. Second, the information about the article or book itself is kept. Third, a list of valid keywords is placed in file. Yes, keywords, which means you can quickly search for all the articles dealing with Visual Basic, or with Serial Communications, in a simple move.

Now the only problem will be getting someone to enter all the data for those tags you've collected.

All of the programs in this book run under Windows. This will help you make a permanent move into the environment, because there are fewer and fewer reasons to drop out to DOS. But for those times when it's still necessary, I present a program called Imposter.

Imposter, shown in Figure 2-15, is a DOS shell program, basically a Windows program that looks like the good old DOS C: prompt. Imposter isn't as robust as the DOS shell supplied with Windows, but that's okay.

Figure 2-15. *Imposter looks like the DOS C: prompt, and lets you see what you've been missing by running everything under Windows*

Imposter only uses a fraction of the memory and resources that the DOS window uses. Plus, since it's a real Windows program, it can process while other Windows progams continue to run.

Imposter doesn't support everything that DOS does, but it supports the ability to handle all the internal DOS commands available in DOS 5. This is a good deal of what you might need. For instance, you might want to copy some files while you're working. I know, File Manager could do it too, but Imposter is much less of a resource hog. Besides, sometimes you want to use the command line, just to remind yourself why you moved to Windows in the first place.

Back to Windows now. Despite the fact that DOS is an exciting new technology to be running under Windows, we should get back to the normal things you might do. After all, who has the capability to run DOS anymore anyway?

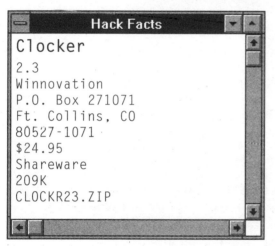

Hack Facts

Clocker
2.3
Winnovation
P.O. Box 271071
Ft. Collins, CO
80527-1071
$24.95
Shareware
209K
CLOCKR23.ZIP

Clocker is a program that has many uses. It can start a process at a given time, which is is quite handy in many situations.

For instance, you may want to save some money by sending faxes via your modem during evening hours when the rates are cheaper. Using Clocker, you could set this up to happen after the rates drop. How about backups? (Of course you do backups, right?) With Clocker, you can have your system back itself up automatically late at night, when you won't need to use it. If you're on a network, each person can set Clocker for a different time, and the server can keep busy all night.

Clocker also has some excellent scheduling options. You can run an application every few minutes, each day, weekly, or monthly. Or you can choose to run it only once. You can create groups of applications, all of which will be handled together. Naturally, you can log all the executions to a file, and check what actually happened.

the possibilities here are exciting. I can automatically run a game program at 5:00 pm to remind me to go home, or at least take a break. I can run a time-keeping program at 8:00 am to remind me to check into the project I'm working on. Before long, I'll really be able to work all day and night, and the computer will make sure I get the right things done. What a concept!

Editors for Programmers

One of the most important tools a programmer uses is the text editor. If you're a programmer working in a professional software development environment, you may not have a choice in the editor you use. Most of the newer compilers come with their own editors. Until recently, though, these editors were all DOS-based.

So if you're still using a DOS editor, and have the option to move ahead, this section is for you.

Hack Facts

InfView
1.44
Dean Software Design
P.O. Box 2331
Everett, WA
98203-0331
$6.99
Shareware
276K
INFVU144.ZIP

In any case, InfView, shown in Figure 2-16, is a great utility to have in addition to your regular editor. InfView is used to view files (of any size, they claim) in text or hexadecimal mode. Guess what? The hex display looks a lot like the old DOS Debug screen (hex on the left, text down the right). I still think this is the most effective way to view a file in hex, but it doesn't cease to amaze me how much Windows programs look like DOS programs.

InfView doesn't allow you to edit the files it views. But it's very useful when your application generates large report files, or dated logs, or other large data files. Again, it doesn't matter if it is text or binary; InfView will show them both.

InfView has some nice options. You can execute the file once you have viewed it. You can select a font for and the size of your viewing area. You can print the file. You can even search the disk for files, by name or by their contents (like, "Find all the files that have 'Microsoft' embedded in them").

```
┌─────────────────────────────────────────────────────────────────┐
│ ─         Viewing: C:\AUTOEXEC.BAT <unregistered>          ▼ ▲   │
├─────────────────────────────────────────────────────────────────┤
│  File  Edit  Search  View  Options  Print  Execute  Help         │
├─────────────────────────────────────────────────────────────────┤
│ Line:   1 File Size:   1843 chars / 0000:0733 hex            ▲    │
│ 0000:0000 40  45  43  48  4F  20  4F  46  46  0D  0A  43  3A  5C  57  49 | @ECHO OFF..C:\WI │
│ 0000:0010 4E  44  4F  57  53  5C  6E  65  74  20  73  74  61  72  74  0D | NDOWS\net start. │
│ 0000:0020 0A  4C  48  20  2F  4C  3A  31  2C  31  36  39  34  34  20  43 | .LH /L:1,16944 C │
│ 0000:0030 3A  5C  44  4F  53  5C  53  48  41  52  45  20  2F  4C  3A  35 | :\DOS\SHARE /L:5 │
│ 0000:0040 30  30  20  2F  46  3A  35  31  30  30  0D  0A  72  65  6D  20 | 00 /F:5100..rem  │
│ 0000:0050 4C  48  20  2F  4C  3A  31  2C  33  36  32  32  34  20  43  3A | LH /L:1,36224 C: │
│ 0000:0060 5C  44  4F  53  5C  6D  73  63  64  65  78  2E  65  78  65  20 | \DOS\mscdex.exe  │
│ 0000:0070 2F  64  3A  6D  76  63  64  30  30  31  20  2F  6D  3A  31  30 | /d:mvcd001 /m:10 │
│ 0000:0080 20  2F  76  0D  0A  4C  48  20  2F  4C  3A  31  2C  32  33  34 | /v..LH /L:1,234 │
│ 0000:0090 30  38  20  63  3A  5C  76  72  61  6D  5C  75  74  69  6C  5C | 08 c:\vram\util\ │
│ 0000:00A0 73  6D  6F  64  65  20  6D  6F  6E  69  74  6F  72  0D  0A  4C | smode monitor..L │
│ 0000:00B0 48  20  2F  4C  3A  30  3B  31  2C  34  35  34  38  38  20  2F | H /L:0;1,45488 / │
│ 0000:00C0 53  20  43  3A  5C  57  49  4E  44  4F  57  53  5C  53  4D  41 | S C:\WINDOWS\SMA │
│ 0000:00D0 52  54  44  52  56  2E  45  58  45  0D  0A  69  66  20  5B  25 | RTDRV.EXE..if [% │
│ 0000:00E0 63  6F  6E  66  69  67  25  5D  3D  5B  6E  6F  5F  63  64  72 | config%]=[no_cdr │
│ 0000:00F0 6F  6D  5D  20  67  6F  74  6F  20  73  6B  69  70  5F  63  64 | om] goto skip_cd │
│ 0000:0100 0D  0A  4C  48  20  2F  4C  3A  31  2C  33  36  32  32  34  20 | ..LH /L:1,36224  │
│ 0000:0110 43  3A  5C  57  49  4E  44  4F  57  53  5C  4D  53  43  44  45 | C:\WINDOWS\MSCDE │
│ 0000:0120 58  2E  45  58  45  20  2F  53  20  2F  56  20  2F  45  20  2F | X.EXE /S /V /E / ▼│
│ ◀ ▮                                                          ▶   │
└─────────────────────────────────────────────────────────────────┘
```

Figure 2-16.   *InfView lets you view a file in text or hex notation. Looks like DOS again, don't you think?*

Hack Facts

SCFile

2.0
Software Assist Corp.
75 Maryland Ave. South
Golden Valley, MN
55426-1544
$25
Shareware
154K
SCFILE.ZIP

Another file viewer to discuss is SCFile. The company claims that SCFile can read and display a file of approximately 1,000,000,000 bytes. No, I wasn't able to test this; all the computers in my office put together can't handle a file that big. This is also supposed to be just as fast as viewing a 100 byte file. SCFile *is* fast, but again, this test couldn't be done.

SCFile is different from InfView in that it doesn't do hex mode. It does, however, allow selected words to be displayed in another color. This is useful, for example, in finding all the records in an address file from a specific city. It can also be used to locate all the occurrences of a variable name in source code.

For Visual Basic programmers, there is an additional feature available. You can display Visual Basic arrays of any size in an SCFile window. This allows for a quick method of checking the VB arrays, without writing much code at all.

```
┌─────────────────────────────────┐
│ ─  │     Hack Facts      │ ▼ ▲ │
├─────────────────────────────────┤
│ E! for Windows              │ ▲ │
│ 1.20G                       │   │
│ HomeBrew Software           │   │
│ 807 Davis St.               │   │
│ Vacaville, CA  95687        │   │
│ $108                        │   │
│ Shareware                   │   │
│ 1,110K                      │   │
│ EWARC.ZIP,                  │   │
│ EWCT3D.ZIP                  │ ▼ │
├─────────────────────────────────┤
│ ◄ │                       │ ► │
└─────────────────────────────────┘
```

When you get into the actual editing, you'll want to look at E! for Windows and Mega Edit. These are two of the more popular editors available in Windows, both designed with programmers in mind.

E! for Windows is a full-featured development environment for programmers in Windows (EWARC is the editor and EWCT3D is the 3-D controls add-on). Not only is it an editor, it has available (for registered users) a full API. This means that you can write your own add-ons to the package, maybe adding features you always had in your DOS editor, but were afraid to ask for under Windows.

I won't go into these editors too deeply, because there are literally hundreds of features available in both of them. Of course, full online help is available. E! is probably best suited for programming, with built-in menu selections for running your compiler, and performing other programming tasks not present in most text editors.

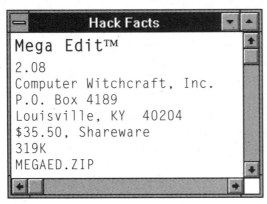

```
┌─────────────────────────────────┐
│ ─  │     Hack Facts      │ ▼ ▲ │
├─────────────────────────────────┤
│ Mega Edit™                  │ ▲ │
│ 2.08                        │   │
│ Computer Witchcraft, Inc.   │   │
│ P.O. Box 4189               │   │
│ Louisville, KY  40204       │   │
│ $35.50, Shareware           │   │
│ 319K                        │   │
│ MEGAED.ZIP                  │ ▼ │
├─────────────────────────────────┤
│ ◄ │                       │ ► │
└─────────────────────────────────┘
```

Again, both of these text editors are designed with programmers in mind, but E! more so than Mega Edit.

Mega Edit is a wonderful editing package for all your text processing needs. You can use it quickly, without the overhead of large editing systems ("word processors," which require "big processors") or in-depth compiler environments. You can edit a file of nearly any length (I haven't found any that don't work), can change the color scheme to match your office or your shirt, and can do a search faster than many programs running under DOS.

Mega Edit is a superior replacement for the Notepad, for all text editing tasks. It's fast, simple to use, and very robust. If you already have a text editor, or programming environment, Mega Edit is a good all-purpose editor for those quick tasks you need to perform. It loads quickly, acts quickly, and gets out of the way when you are finished.

Finishing Up

We're almost finished with the programmer's assistants that are available on the CD-ROM in this book. You've probably found that some of them are more helpful than others, and some are just there for fun. But before we go on to real programming stuff (source code, libraries, the typical buzzwords), there are two more utilities to discover.

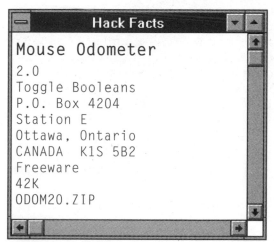

```
Hack Facts

Mouse Odometer
2.0
Toggle Booleans
P.O. Box 4204
Station E
Ottawa, Ontario
CANADA   K1S 5B2
Freeware
42K
ODOM20.ZIP
```

Ask your computer reseller for the mileage warranty on your mouse.

The first one is Mouse Odometer. You might not know it, but you *need* this program. It tells you approximately how much you've moved your mouse. Is this useful? Of course!

Let's say you're designing a graphical front end for a client. They don't believe you've spent much time on it and don't want to pay you. Sorry, you tell them, here's the documented proof that I've taken the mouse for a trip of over four miles in the last few days. The work has been done.

This goes for your boss, too. If he or she thinks you aren't working, show the mileage on your mouse. Maybe you could charge by the inch, rather than by the hour. Maybe mouse products could start coming with a 500 mile or 500 day warranty. Then, you'd need to know the tracking units per inch you might expect, when you'd need to change the rubber on the ball, what type of mouse pad would make for better wear and longer life, and how to manage the use of a trackball or joystick as a replacement.

Maybe not. But in any case, Mouse Odometer is a fun tool. It can show the current odometer in inches, feet, miles, etc. It can update nearly continuously, or just every so often. Play with it. Then if you get sore wrists, you'll know it's because of the mileage.

Hack Facts

```
Alvida
1.0
Tej K. Dhawan
Dhawan Computer Consulting
5233 Walnut St.
West Des Moines, IA  50265
$5 or a utility program
   you wrote
Shareware
48K
ALVIDA.ZIP
```

The final program for this chapter is called Alvida. It's a quick way to get out of Windows. And it has some options not available in other similar programs.

For instance, there are several programs that let you quickly leave Windows (VBSystem, mentioned earlier, has this option). Some even have the ability to restart Windows immediately. But Alvida adds a third, very useful option: Rebooting the computer.

Have you ever had a program lock up? I'm sure you haven't under Windows, but I know I've heard that it happens. You press CTRL-ALT-DEL, and are greeted by a text-based Windows screen, giving you the reason why your program has gone south. Usually, it's "system is unstable," or "application is refusing to respond to Windows," or something in that vein.

If you already know the program is hosed, this extra reminder doesn't help. If you don't reboot, Windows may not run well again anyway. So just call up Alvida, and tell it you want to reboot the computer. That's it. No pesky reassurance screens. It's a virtual Big Red Button (also known as the power switch).

I think I like this program the most because it gets around the Windows handlers. That's fun. It lets you do the things you want to do without being told how to do them (or making you confirm your decisions many times over). This is sounding more and more like DOS...

Edit
Tip
Quote

The kings of modern thought are dumb.
—Matthew Arnold

Hacking Ahead

In this chapter, we talked about some tools you can use in your nonprogramming tasks. In the next couple of chapters, you'll learn about some tools specifically designed for your programming hours, all twenty-five of them per day.

Before you go on, though, hit the CD-ROM, and try out some of the things we talked about here. You'll really enjoy the new freedom you feel, as you start back into programming topics.

2

Language-Free and Language-Specific

There's good news and bad news about shareware code for Windows programmers. The good news is that it still exists. In fact, more and more software is becoming available. Environments like Visual Basic are making it possible for people who didn't used to be programmers to become programmers. This can be an exciting change; many people with good program ideas didn't have the time, knowledge, or patience to write programs or hire a programmer. Now, with a little training, they can write applications in Visual Basic.

Of course, I don't advocate a shift to the world of Visual Basic for everyone. It's a wonderful development environment, but the execution is somewhat slower, and it's BASIC! That's part of the bad news.

My job title was computer. Other people have programmed computers, but I have been one.
—C. Wayne Ratliff

The other part is that Microsoft has made it easier to not supply source code. When you wrote programs and libraries for DOS, it was easy to give out source code. After all, if you wanted to use the library with any known compiler or memory model, you would expect to recompile it. It was easier for a programmer to give out the source than to try to prebuild all the different library combinations.

No longer! With the advent of Dynamic Link Libraries (DLLs), and a common programming interface, you can give out a DLL and not worry about the language that someone will be using.

There are two separate chapters about programming tools. This chapter covers those tools which do not include source code (some might, with a higher registration fee). In Chapter 4, you'll find out about the tools still available that include source code.

Too Much Work Makes Jack a DLL Boy

The first place to start then is with some of the DLLs that are available. Don't work so hard if you don't have to! These DLLs are already done, and included in this book for you to try!

These DLLs should be useful for programmers using any Windows-based language. If you're a beginning Visual Basic programmer, however, realize that these might take some extra work, because they are not VBX-based, and therefore don't fit immediately into the environment.

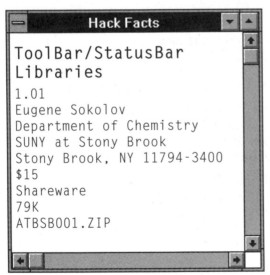

Hack Facts

ToolBar/StatusBar
Libraries
1.01
Eugene Sokolov
Department of Chemistry
SUNY at Stony Brook
Stony Brook, NY 11794-3400
$15
Shareware
79K
ATBSB001.ZIP

This package is a good place to start the discussion of DLLs. It consists of two libraries used to assist your program in generating a toolbar and a status bar. Toolbars are those groups of tiny little icons you see at the top, side, or bottom of many Windows applications. A status bar is placed at the bottom of the window, and provides a convenient location for status messages (of course) to be shown.

There are many options for these toolbars. For instance, you can move the toolbar around or fix it to one location. You can also choose whether or not to place a border around the buttons, as shown in Figure 3-1.

Buttons on the toolbar can be simple push buttons (push it and it goes down, then comes back up on its own) or they can be two-state buttons (push it and it goes down, then push it again for it to come back up). They can also be two-state, but related to other buttons (like the idea behind

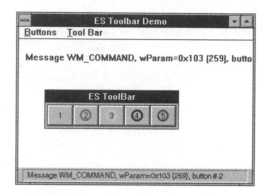

Figure 3-1. *The demo program lets you try out all the options. Now your programs can have these tiny icons too!*

radio buttons); if you push a button, the other buttons all come up automatically.

The status bar is called like a **printf( )** statement (C-language function that writes data out to the screen). You can use this to let your users know what's going on in your program. It's also handy for debugging.

Some of the newer compilers are including features for adding toolbars and status bars. But if you'd like a language-independent method, this little DLL is for you.

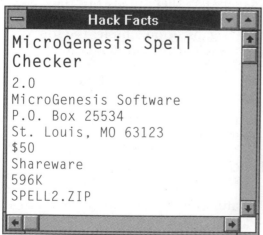

MicroGenesis Spell Checker
2.0
MicroGenesis Software
P.O. Box 25534
St. Louis, MO 63123
$50
Shareware
596K
SPELL2.ZIP

Spell Checker is another DLL that can be used in your programs. The Spell Checker package comes complete with examples in Visual Basic and C, so you don't have to think too hard to put the library into use.

This DLL is a spelling checker. Sure, not everyone needs a spelling cheker (oops, I mean checker). After all, can you imagine a graphic, spreadsheet, or CAD drawing that had *words* in it? And besides, Spell Checker would only be useful if people *actually* misspelled words, right?

Complicated programs are far easier to write than straightforward programs.

—John Page

Well, since this is probably the case more often than not, you should look into Spell Checker as an option to add to your programs. This package comes with two dictionaries. The first one is supplied for maximum coverage, and covers over 119,000 words, using around 400K of disk space. A smaller one is supplied for those programs that may be floppy disk-based (59,000 words in 230K of disk space).

Using Spell Checker, you can look up words, add words to the dictionary, ask for suggested spellings, and do all this from C, C++, Pascal, or Visual Basic. Other languages that support DLLs should also work fine.

be sure to register this one if you plan to release a program that uses it; it's required by the license, and you'll receive full source code for the library!

This next tool may not be as universally required, but it's very handy for any programs that require the user to create an organized list or outline.

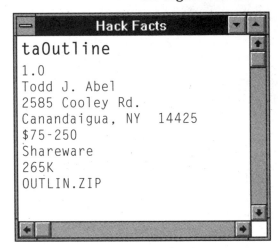

Hack Facts

taOutline

1.0
Todd J. Abel
2585 Cooley Rd.
Canandaigua, NY   14425
$75-250
Shareware
265K
OUTLIN.ZIP

taOutline, shown in Figure 3-2, is a DLL that creates and manages an outline tool. Outlines have a variety of purposes; word processors use them for structuring documents, presentation packages use them for planning slide sequences, information managers use them to lay out the things that have to be done. This makes organization simple: the top level of the outline could be the month, the next level the day, and the lower levels the different items that have to be done for the day.

As I said, this may not be as universally required as a spell checker, but presents a lot of possibilities. The examples are provided in C and Visual C++. Full source code is available, if you can afford the high end of the registration fee.

By the way, the numbering and indenting can be turned off with this outline control, giving you a basic list manager. Another exciting possibility: getting two tools for the price

```
┌──────────────────────────────────────────────────┐
│ ─  │        Test Windows Application - Test    │ ▼ ▲ │
├──────────────────────────────────────────────────┤
│ Outline  Help                                      │
├──────────────────────────────────────────────────┤
│ 1. Item Top Level                    │             │
│    1.1. Sub Item 1                   │             │
│    1.2.│Another Indented One│        │             │
│ 2. Second Top Level Item             │             │
│                                      │             │
│                                      │             │
│                                      │             │
│                                      │             │
│                                      │             │
│                                      │             │
│                                      │             │
├──────────────────────────────────────────────────┤
│ Setting focus to the second outline control │ NUM │
└──────────────────────────────────────────────────┘
```

Figure 3-2. *Outline makes it simple to add organization capabilities to your programs*

of one! Even if you don't need an outliner, most programs can use some sort of list from time to time.

```
┌──────────────────────────────────┐
│ ─        Hack Facts        ▼ ▲  │
├──────────────────────────────────┤
│ WinDES                        ▲  │
│ Controlled Information           │
│ Environments                     │
│ P.O. Box 457                     │
│ La Mesa, CA                      │
│ 91944-0457                       │
│ $15                              │
│ Shareware (corporations)         │
│ Freeware (individuals)           │
│ 45K                              │
│ WINDES.ZIP                    ▼  │
├──────────────────────────────────┤
│ ◄                            ►  │
└──────────────────────────────────┘
```

Another interesting DLL you may wish to consider is WinDES, a data encryption module. This library is freeware to noncommercial beings (those not trying to make money from it). "Honest" business users, according to the documentation, may purchase a license for their entire site for only $15. Is this a deal or what!

What does WinDES do? It encrypts and decrypts (codes and decodes, messes up and straightens out) data, using a key that you provide. Don't forget the key! Part of the purpose for the Data Encryption Standard is to make ciphers (hidden things) hard to figure out. If you really want to get technical, DES is defined by the ANSI Standard X3.92-1981.

How does WinDES work? Does it matter? There's a lot that goes on within this library to generate the coded or decoded data, none of which matters to me as long as no one can read what I don't want them to read. If you really want to know more, you'll probably want to register this software and then order a copy of the pertinent ANSI standard.

This can be very useful in hiding setup data, encoding database entries, or hiding other information from prying eyes. And if they try to look, our next DLL may provide an interesting manner of handling the intrusion.

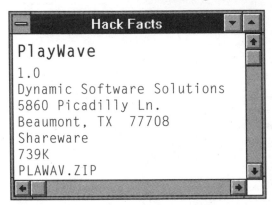

```
Hack Facts

PlayWave
1.0
Dynamic Software Solutions
5860 Picadilly Ln.
Beaumont, TX  77708
Shareware
739K
PLAWAV.ZIP
```

PlayWave is a shareware version of a complete multimedia library. Its purpose is to simplify the process of playing WAV (sound) files in Windows. So if your user does something stupid, tell them about it! Prerecord some sayings of the moment, and let PlayWave handle production of the sound at the right times. Another use for PlayWave is with shareware programs in asking for registrations (or donations)! For instance, I can see a CD player program that says "Please register this software" after every CD. After all, if they are playing CDs, you know they must have sound capabilities. Then, when they register, send a version that simply says "Thanks for your registration" once, and from then on keeps quiet so the music can play.

Here's an example of an entire Windows program in C++ code that plays two different sounds.

```
Edit
 Tip
 Quote
```

Most organizations don't set out consciously to kill teams. They just act that way.
—Tome DeMarco and Timothy Lister

```
#include "playwave.hpp"
PLAYWAVE PlayWave;
int PASCAL WinMain(HANDLE hInstance,
          HANDLE hPrevInstance,
          LPSTR lpstrCmdLine,
          int nCmdShow)
}
  PlayWave.Resource(hInstance,"SOUND");
  PlayWave.Play("SPOCKD.WAV",SOUND_SYNC);

}
```

The first sound is played with the **PlayWave.Resource( )** call. In this call, the file that is to be played is read from the resource file, using the name "SOUND." This is ideal; when you add foreign language capabilities to your programs, you can now add foreign language verbal insults right along in the resource file. That way, no one has to feel that they're getting less than the complete package!

Using the **PlayWave.Play( )** call, any filename can be supplied. This is good for those programs that do not need to change their sound effects. In a game program, rocket boosters will sound the same in any language, so why worry about changes?

GetYour$ helps you gather all the information you need for your program registrations. This is a Visual Basic program, with all you need to:

- Mention to the user that they are using a shareware package, which needs to be registered

- Allow the user to enter pertinent information into an order form, which can then be printed

- Accept the registration code from the user

- Turn off shareware reminders, or turn on features, once the registration code is verified

Adding GetYour$, shown in Figure 3-3, to your programs makes collection of registrations much simpler. And for the fee charged for this package, you can't go wrong. See, Visual Basic programmers, I didn't leave you out! The only problem with this offering is that it is *only* for Visual Basic. That's okay, though. I'm sure the hardy C, C++, and Pascal programmers can figure this one out, using the examples provided. Besides, there are other products available for them.

Figure 3-3. *GetYour$ gives you a program registration form and will even print the form when completed*

ShareWare Tools is one such product. This is a package designed for Pascal programmers (and written in Pascal) that includes a DLL. This means that we die-hard C and C++ programmers have a challenge to call this from our programs, since the functions are very worthwhile.

There are several tools in this package. First, there is a scramble function (also available as a demonstration program), that takes a name and password, and creates a scrambled key. This key is made up of ANSI characters, but is certainly not readable. The theory is that you can use this to scramble all sorts of things that need to be stored in files.

One feature included is the ability to time-stamp your program, telling it to expire after a certain number of days. You write the installation date, scrambled of course, to a disk file. At any time, you can determine the number of days the program has been in use, and know when it expires.

Here again is a universal package that might help in ways you thought you didn't have time to worry about. Putting an expiration date on a program turns it into a very effective demonstration version, without having to track a second copy of the code.

When the user finally enters the correct code (which, we hope, they got from you after paying a lot of big bucks), you can store something pertinent in the data file, still scrambled, and allow them full use of the program.

With the DLLs discussed above, you have a great deal of functionality that can be added to your programs with minimal effort. Now, since we're doing Windows programming, is there anything that makes the development process itself a little simpler? Read on.

Watching Inside Your Program

One of the simplest ways to debug DOS programs is to add some sort of printing (**printf( )**, **Write( )**, PRINT, etc.) at pertinent points. This allows you a quick check on what's happening. In Windows, however, this is not as simple. You have to watch where your windows are, what they are doing, and where your print statement's output would end up. The tools in this section may help; don't forget that the ToolBar/StatusBar program presented earlier in this chapter also offers some hope.

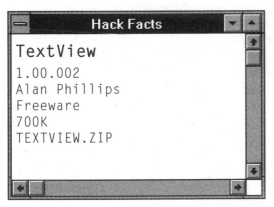

TextView is an excellent package for debugging code under Windows. Beyond debugging, it has many uses in regular program generation.

TextView, shown in Figure 3-4, is a DLL that manages one or more logging windows. Each window can receive text messages from your program. In this way, you get the benefit of the print statements you used in DOS, without the mess you might expect.

3

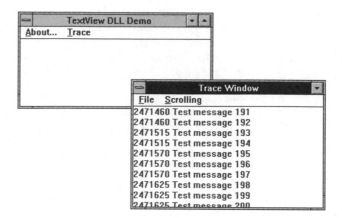

Figure 3-4.   *TextView lets you watch what your programs are doing. It's even better than **printf( )!***

Each of the windows can be set up with automatic or manual scrolling. In automatic mode, the messages just continue to scroll off the screen as they are received. Don't worry, though, because if you switch to manual mode, you can use the scroll bar to back up to the messages that have flown by.

Since this scroll window is maintained outside your program, there are some other nice features you can exploit. Each message can be time stamped, and you can change the colors of the messages. This is extremely neat when you have multiple processes you are trying to make work together. One process uses blue, one uses red, and the third uses black. Since each message is time stamped (if you so specified), you can now see exactly what is happening in all three applications from a single logging window!

this may still be a lot of work, especially if the messages are concentrated in one place in the code, and they come fast and furious. If this is your case, LogFile, discussed next, may be a better solution.

```
Hack Facts

LogFile
1.0
Matthew Raffel
3101 Treelodge Pkwy.
Dunwoody, GA  30350
$10-15
Shareware
42K
LGFIL1.ZIP
```

LogFile performs a similar function to TextView, but places all the messages into a disk file. In this way, you can go peruse the data at your leisure, long after the program has ended its test.

This is a good tool for training and documentation, too. By logging all the functions that are performed in your program, you can explain and document all the tasks and in what order they occur. In multitasking programs, especially, this can be a real lifesaver; you can quickly see in what order tasks occur, and determine if there are timing problems caused by the many tasks.

LogFile was originally developed for Visual Basic programmers, but the source is available in Borland C++. This should make it easy enough to use with any of the DLL-capable languages. There are no example programs included, but the documentation shows how simple it is to use the three functions (open the log file, write to it, and close it). There is not much work or understanding required to get this one to execute as desired.

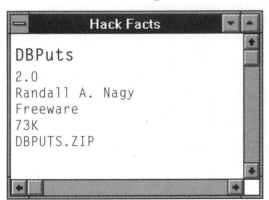

```
Hack Facts

DBPuts
2.0
Randall A. Nagy
Freeware
73K
DBPUTS.ZIP
```

DBPuts is another Windows debugging system, originally described in the "Some Assembly Required" column of the December 1992 issue of *BYTE* magazine. Randall Nagy says he wrote the article to help explain how DLLs work in general, and how to use DBPuts in particular.

DBPuts comes with three pertinent pieces. The DBPuts DLL file manages the passing of messages from the DBClient process to the DBServer process.

3

Generally, you can use the DBServer as is, to receive messages from any number of processes. Each of these processes will be patterned after the DBClient program that's included. Source code is provided for both of these tools, so it's not a problem to change how they work. In fact, I would have said that there are fewer features here than with TextView, but if you can play with the source (as most programmers can), you may find this an even more intriguing package. Also, this one is actually free!

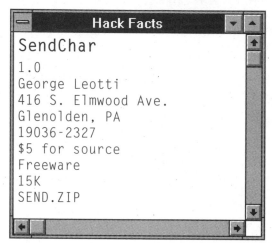

```
Hack Facts

SendChar

1.0
George Leotti
416 S. Elmwood Ave.
Glenolden, PA
19036-2327
$5 for source
Freeware
15K
SEND.ZIP
```

One final entry in this group is somewhat different—thus far, we've been discussing ways to output debugging messages. SendChar is used to enter keystrokes into your program. Do you see the connection?

SendChar has a lot of uses with or without being in debug mode. For instance, you can create your own macros using SendChar. Perhaps there is a function in your program that requires a number of keystrokes, and you want to be able to perform them with one keypress. Rather than rewrite your program to handle both methods of entry, use SendChar to send the appropriate "old" keystrokes to your program when the user presses the "new" key.

SendChar is very versatile, in that it allows you to send both the press and release state of the key. Therefore, you can automatically press down the SHIFT key, for instance, while some task is occurring. This makes all the input uppercase without you having to perform any conversions.

SendChar is also a useful tool for writing automated test scripts. If you put a series of commands in a file, for instance, your application can read the file, determine the key to be pressed, use SendChar to press the key (or release it), and then let the program respond, all without a user's intervention. This is a great way to try a function a hundred times without sitting at the keyboard to do it.

Better Than the Average Listing

Possibly the best tool in debugging is a clean, accurate program listing. This is an area where Windows has finally met and exceeded the capabilities that DOS provided. Most of the newer compilers, and the programs we'll discuss next, allow the use of fonts and character attributes (bold, italic, underline) in your listings, making code much more readable.

Even if TheLister didn't do anything, I'd probably include it here just for the beauty of the screens used in its design (as an example, see Figure 3-5). I know, I know, we're all supposed to look the same, so the neophytes can catch on more quickly. But what's wrong with a little excitement?

TheLister is a program designed to print Pascal source code listings. It can be used for other languages, but the keyword management, comments, etc., will not print the way you might expect.

I guess most of the program listers are that way. The language or languages they cover print beautifully, and the rest of the files just

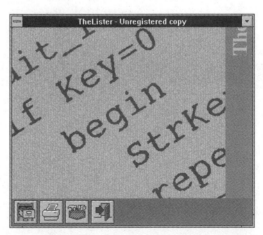

Figure 3-5. *Just an example of some of the great design used in TheLister*

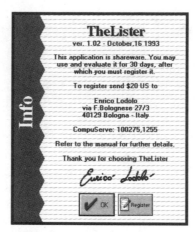

Figure 3-6. *Even in its opening screen, TheLister shows a flair for the exciting*

print. That's okay; it's still a far cry from heading out to the DOS shell to use the PRINT statement. Remember, when you use the DOS shell, if you go back to your work, the shell will stop printing! Unless you have moved up to Windows NT, the DOS shell cannot multitask, and will therefore stop printing if you stop paying attention to it.

As I was saying, TheLister has some of the most pleasing screens I have seen in any program, not just in shareware! The images here look good, but wait until you see them in color. Notice in the main menu screen, shown in Figure 3-6, there are still simple buttons for the user. I like it!

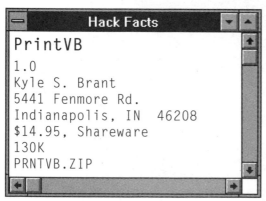

Visual Basic has become a very popular programming environment for Windows. But because it is so different from other programming environments, there come challenges. One of these is how to print everything out in a unified manner. There are forms, attributes, objects, and even source code! Our second entry in the printout category is called PrintVB, and it performs wonderfully.

You can quickly print the forms, source code, attributes, or any combination of these from any of your programs. It doesn't take long to get started, and you get very impressive results. This is a great aid in debugging, and in final program documentation.

No discussion of printing programs would be complete if there wasn't at least one that could handle any language equally as well. CodePrint, shown in Figure 3-7, is a printing program for any ASCII text files printed under Windows.

Now, this isn't like the DOS PRINT command, where you have to fit everything you want on the command line, where you have a limit to the number of files you can print at once (so wildcards don't always help too much), or where your only options are whether to print or not. CodePrint offers a full selection of fonts and character sizes, number of columns to print per page, headers and footers, and other features usually associated with word processing or document preparation programs.

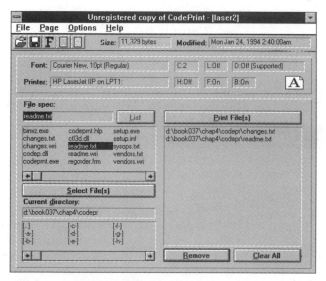

Figure 3-7. *CodePrint handles all your printing needs through a single dialog*

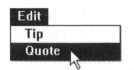

What we anticipate seldom occurs; what we least expect generally happens.
—Benjamin Disraeli

Once you find a group of settings you like, you can save the configuration for later use. And selecting files to print couldn't be much easier. Simply point to the files you want, and build a list until you can't pick anymore. The files can be pulled from any drives and directories on your system. All of this through simple point and click movements.

If you want to print code listings, two across, on pages oriented horizontally (or landscape, for your documentation people) using a really tiny font, you can do so with little change. Add your company name and copyright to the footer, the filename, date, and page number to the header. Now you're talking a serious program listing. Does this one beat DOS? You bet! This isn't just for programmers either. Any text file is fair game for processing and printing by CodePrint.

Managing All That Data

There are a number of standard database systems being thrown at programmers right now. Do you want dBase or Paradox compatibility? Client-server? Should you be migrating to SQL? Whose network will your server support? What if you don't have the right language for the preprocessor?

What if you just want to write a program? I don't know about you, but unless I'm using the Access engine under Visual Basic, there are too many standards and too much money involved with picking the "right" database manager. Here are some simple solutions that allow you to write a program now and maybe worry about the standards later.

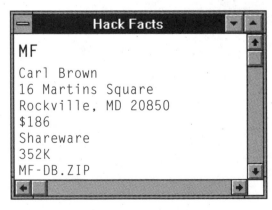

MF is a database manager for Windows. It comes complete with examples for both Visual Basic and C. The program has a subtitle that just begs for inquisition, "Severe-performance database for professional applications." Really. The database manager is designed for the professional programmer looking for high-speed data access, not for the user looking for a simple way to write reports.

MF does support client-server functionality. According to the documentation, MF should perform from 100% to 20,000% faster than many other databases. They haven't tested them all (and neither have I), but the carrot is there for you to try it yourself!

one of the most unique things about MF is its license policy. The next few paragraphs are taken from the documentation:

"MF takes a unique approach to how it is sold: It's $2.

"However, that doesn't mean you own it. It only means you can use it without paying for the distribution rights. The near free status ONLY applies to individuals, small companies and United States federal, state, and local governmental agencies. You may use MF while developing a product for near free. Once you sell your product, you must pay for MF. Note: If you never intend to create a product with MF (e.g. just want to use it for in-house development), please keep in mind that you must pay for distribution rights if you plan to distribute it in-house.

"We aren't trying to be grinches, but it does cost us a heck of a lot to provide tech support.

"Since we are a small company, we understand how difficult it is to start out. We want you to use MF until you create your product and get off the ground. Once you get going, we expect you to pay for MF. Distributing MF with the intention to turn a profit is illegal if you have not registered for the distribution rights.

"In as much, while you are first starting out, you may DISTRIBUTE MF to potential clients at no cost. When you get your first 'pay check' for something created using MF, we expect you to pay the following:

Unlimited Distribution rights: $186

"That said, we also understand that others create 'shareware' at little or no cost. If you create a shareware package and can't afford to pay the registration fee, you may pay a portion of it. As your revenues increase, you can pay any remaining portion of the fee. Our intention is to make an

3

affordable database for you to use. Not make it impossible to create something nifty. In return for the 'time payment plan', we ask for a 'registered' copy of your shareware. (We like nifty things, too!)"

This is a great way to sell your wares, and the real meaning of shareware, if you ask me. This company is working with other companies to get even more software out, which is how the industry can grow. If you need a database manager for your application, here's a company that should get your support just for the good feeling they are spreading.

By the way, if you can't swing the $2, they'll accept a postcard from your hometown as an alternative payment method (remember, they probably already have some "generic" ones).

```
Hack Facts

FLAT
1.0
Dennis R. Fischer
Denam Systems
1115 Madison St. NE
Suite 226
Salem, OR  97303
Freeware
214K
FLAT.ZIP
```

Now that you've heard about MF, why would you ever care about another shareware database manager? Well, FLAT is a flat-file database that has other features you might find useful. For instance, FLAT comes with full source code. And, it's free! These are two good reasons to take a look.

Of course, even free stuff with little use would not be much of a value. FLAT, on the other hand, has some other interesting routines that are worth looking into, even if you don't need the database manager. The source shows how to perform linked-list sorts and data searches, use horizontally scrolling list boxes, and access the WIN.INI file, and presents methods of allocating memory under Windows.

This is a good place to start for a Windows programmer, if you haven't had a lot of experience with some of these items (WIN.INI, for instance). I also like Dennis's quote in the README file: "While you are looking through the FLAT code, you may notice parts you do not agree with or feel it could be done better. If so, change it. It is not going to hurt my feelings. This code is free for the taking and you can do with it, as you want."

I did mention that support wasn't one of the strong suits of freeware offerings, didn't I?

Your Toolkit Shouldn't Be Without These

There are some utilities you'll use for programming and testing that aren't really code-related. Some of the stuff that was mentioned in Chapter 2 falls into this category, but most of those were for nonprogramming tasks. Now that we want to program, here are some nice additions to your toolkit (toolkits for your toolkit?).

```
Hack Facts

Tools
1.0
Arron Davies
P.O. Box 82
West Ryde NSW 2114
AUSTRALIA
$10
Shareware
254K
TOOLS.ZIP
```

The Tools package is a group of utilities, all bundled under a single menu, that helps you in designing and testing your software. There are stress testers, charts, file finders, rulers, and resource trackers. Sounds like a lot for $10, doesn't it?

The stress testers tie up Windows resources, so you can test how well your program does in limited resource situations. You can test for disk space, file handles, global memory, GDI memory, or user memory shortages. You can also track the resources, just to see how they are doing as your application runs.

There are full ANSI, OEM, and Symbol character set charts. An RGB color dialog helps define colors using the separate red, green, and blue values. There is even a hex-to-decimal converter.

If you're defining screens and windows, you'll really like the three tools that are left in this package. First, as shown in Figure 3-8, there's a resizable window that tells you where it's located on the screen, and its current size. This is ideal when you're trying to get your opening window to come up where *you* want, and not where *it* wants. Second, there's a screen coordinate tool that allows you to move the mouse and determine the x and y positions of where the mouse stopped. Third, there's a set of vertical and horizontal ruler windows that can be moved around the screen and used for precise positioning of whatever you want to place, wherever

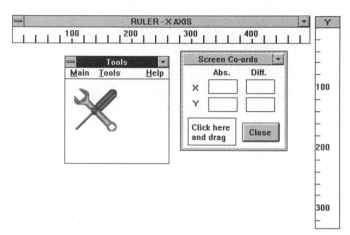

Figure 3-8. The tools in Tools help you determine where everything is on your screen, or where it should be

you want to place it. All of these add up to great time savers when you are trying to design a front end for your latest award-winning applications.

If you use regular expressions, and liked GREP in Unix or under DOS, you'll really like Windows Grep, shown in Figure 3-9. There's not much else to say about this one. All the switches and magic you needed with command-line versions of GREP are replaced by a smooth front end in Windows Grep.

If you aren't sure what GREP is, just remember that it stands for Generalized Regular Expression Parser. I talked about it briefly in Chapter 2, in the discussion of WFind, a regular expression file search utility. WFind has good documentation on how GREP parsing works, as does the documentation for Windows Grep. It may seem confusing at first, but if you spend a little time with these documents, and learn the process one step at a time, you'll see how powerful this tool can be.

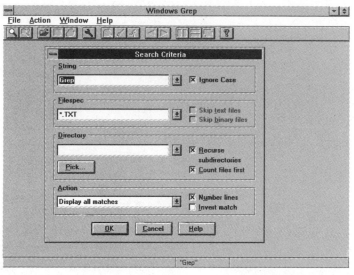

Figure 3-9. *Windows Grep is easy to use and keeps you away from the DOS prompt in one more little way*

3

Hack Facts

Windows Disassembler

1.8
Todd T. Snoddy
4831-7 McCormick
Fort Riley, KS 66442
$39.95
Shareware
302K
WDSM18.ZIP

And finally, we come to our last, most power-hungry programmer utility, the Windows Disassembler, shown in Figure 3-10. What does it do? It takes all that wonderfully understandable code you wrote and painfully compiled into a program, and turns into so much assembly language code.

It's good assembly code, though. It's 486-based, and will run with Microsoft's Macro Assembler (MASM 6.0). And there's even a utility, called HiLevel, that will read in the assembly code and try to create some high-level constructs out of it.

Hopefully, you aren't masochistic enough to want to read the assembly code for all the programs you buy, but if you're using a program from a company that goes out of business,

```
 ─                        Windows Disassembler              ▼ ▲
 File  Edit!  View  Help
Segment 1     is at 5C0          Segment size = 0C514H    D:\WINAPPS\WD ▲
               ADD    BYTE PTR [BX+SI], AL
               ADD    BYTE PTR [BX+SI], AL
               ADD    BYTE PTR [BX+SI], AL
               ADD    BYTE PTR [BX+SI], AL
               ADD    BYTE PTR [BX+SI], AL
               ADD    BYTE PTR [BX+SI], AL
               ADD    BYTE PTR [BX+SI], AL
               ADD    BYTE PTR [BX+SI], AL
               XOR    DX, DX
               XOR    AX, AX
               XOR    SI, SI
               MOV    CL, 4
               JMP    SHORT L005AH
L001AH:        MOV    BL, BYTE PTR [SI+35B4H]
               CMP    BL, 47
               JBE    L002DH
               CMP    BL, 58
               JAE    L002DH
               SUB    BL, 48
               JMP    SHORT L004DH
L002DH:        CMP    BL, 64
               JBE    L003CH
               CMP    BL, 71
               JAE    L003CH
               SUB    BL, 55
               JMP    SHORT L004DH
L003CH:        CMP    BL, 96                                          ▼
```

Figure 3-10.   *Question: What does disassembled code
look like in Windows? Answer: A lot like
disassembled code did under DOS*

and your entire accounting department must either watch
you read assembly code to find the bug or spend $12 million
for new software, this puppy will sure come in handy!

Hacking Ahead

There are a lot of tools available for programmers working in
Windows. You learned about a few of them in this chapter.
Coming up in the next chapter is more of the same, but *all* of
these programs come with source code.

Glass Houses

Source code is a funny thing. Sometimes you think, "I wish I had the source code for this utility/program/hack, so I could see how the programmer did this." I've had that desire, as I'm sure you probably have. There are times when you produce a package, and would like to have the source for a library, so you can rebuild it with the newest versions of your compiler.

On the other hand, there are times when having the source is the worst possible scenario. Has anyone ever told you, "Just change it so we can add this new feature. It won't be hard; you've got the *source code*!" If so, you may want to skip this chapter.

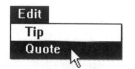

Politicians should read science fiction, not westerns and detective stories.
—*Arthur C. Clarke*

In the last chapter, we talked about DLLs and utilities that save you time in programming. In this chapter, you'll learn more about actual source code snippets that are available. Naturally, these pieces of gold are all in a specific language, but remember that a Windows call is a Windows call, so you should be able to use the ideas from these files in your own work.

Still at the Top of the Charts

I'm back on the music kick again. I know there are already some CD players available, and we even talked about some of them in Chapter 2. But if you get the urge to discover how they work, here is a file for you!

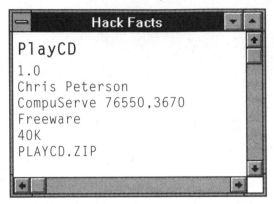

The PlayCD archive contains full source code in C for a CD player.

You may not program in C. In fact, you may be using Visual Basic, and staying as far away from C as possible. That's okay. You can still learn how to make the multimedia calls necessary to start and run an audio CD player from inside Windows.

This isn't the best CD player in the world, mind you. It is, however, fully functional and provides an excellent look at how to manipulate Windows elements, including buttons and the multimedia drivers.

Enough said. I expect to see a good number of CD players on the shareware market soon. One of them will be mine. Will yours be there too?

Would You Like a Date?

One of the functions that everyone tries to write as a programmer (unless they found the code from someone else) is a date manipulation library. How else can you determine when bills are 30 days past due, or when the insurance runs out on someone who is 100 years old? You need to work with dates.

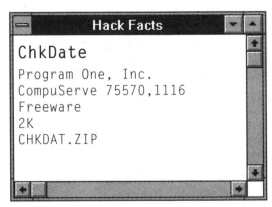

ChkDate is a small routine that is used to validate a date. For instance, when your user enters his or her birth date, and uses the format "02/29/60", do you know whether that date is valid? How about "04/31/94"?

ChkDate takes a date, formatted without the slashes (meaning 040199, rather than 04/01/99), and tells you whether that date is valid. That's all. A simple function to perform a simple function. Pass in a date like "02/29/94", and find out that it is not valid (there is no 29th day of February in 1994).

The source code for ChkDate is written in C.

Hack Facts

Date Validate
1.1
Albert C. Schmitt
CompuServe 70541,2362
Freeware
130K
DVLD11.EXE

There are two packages included on the CD-ROM that manage date functions. Do you need date functions? Possibly, if you want to keep track of birthdays and anniversaries, or you deal with files that have creation dates, invoices with due dates, schedules with starting and ending dates, or any other type of data that revolves around the management of dates.

The first of the packages is called Date Validate. This is a set of routines written in C that handles almost every possible date problem you might have. You can convert a date from Gregorian (that is, the normal calendar system we use) to Julian (where each day is just a single number), and then convert it back from Julian to Gregorian. This is extremely useful in database applications; to reduce storage and processing requirements, simply store the single Julian number in your date field.

Date Validate also includes routines to extract the month, day, and year from a Julian date, without doing them all at once. If you want to see the date in a nice format, you can even convert a Julian date into a text string that is simple to read and display.

Finally, Date Validate has a function that returns the last day of the current month. This is nice for applications where you perform special processing at the end of the month, and don't want to waste time figuring out whether today is actually the last day. With this routine, just compare the current date against the last day of the month, and do the special processing if they match.

Date Validate comes complete with examples for Borland C++, Microsoft Visual C++, and Turbo Pascal for Windows. There are no excuses here for not giving it a chance!

Hack Facts

```
DateMath/DateCalc
1.0
Expertec, Inc.
Attn: Chet Kloss
340 North Main St.
Suite 304
Plymouth, MI  48170
$24.95
Shareware
155K
DATEMA.ZIP
```

DateMath, shown in Figure 4-1, is a similar package, but with a special twist. DateMath has been written with the realization that not everyone works seven days a week. For instance, there are people who only work five or six days a week. After a lot of years with the firm, they are given a day or two of rest each week (usually Saturday or Sunday, since they both start with an *S*, as in *Sleep*).

Other people get holidays off work. To handle these possibilities, DateMath allows you to define a simple calendar, detailing the days off each week ("rest days," they're called) and the dates of the holidays. From this point on, all the calculations you perform take this calendar into account.

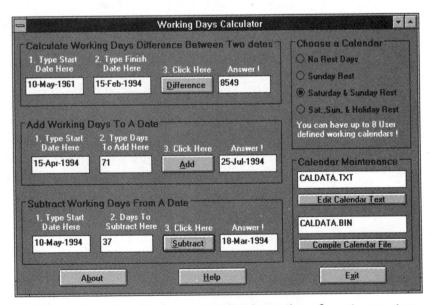

Figure 4-1. *DateMath lets you perform date functions using a customized work calendar*

The radical invents the new ideas, and when he has worn them out the conservative adopts them.

—Mark Twain

DateMath also comes with a complete application that shows the use of the routines included in the library. DateMath doesn't do all the Julian and Gregorian conversions that DateVld performs, but the purposes for its use are quite obvious. With the included routines, you can find the number of days between two dates (taking rest days and holidays into account), or the date that is a number of days before or after another date. Once again, you can perform these searches or calculations based on the full five-, six-, or seven-day workweeks, with or without holidays.

These calculations may not seem immediately useful. But they are already helping in my schedule: if I have a 240-hour project (30 eight-hour days), and I only want to work weekdays (no weekends or holidays), when will I finish? This helps in scheduling and billing the actual work.

Under the Hood

Many of the routines you'll find in this chapter may not have immediate uses. But look through them. Some day you'll need to write a program that does something you haven't done before, and much of the information you need will come directly from these source files.

In this section, we'll talk about some of the source code available to read information about the computer you are using. It is always good to know what kind of machine you are dealing with; Windows hides some of the mundane problems of compatibility from you, but not everything can be generic—what fun would that be?

Hack Facts

```
GetCPU
Cliff Brown
CompuServe 71650,423
Freeware
4K
GETCPU.ZIP
```

GetCPU is a tiny assembly language function that tells you what type of CPU is being used in the computer.

Now, this is another function you may not think you need. But just wait until you write a game program, or try to add some animation to your latest Visual Basic program. By knowing the CPU that your system is using, whether it be a 8086, 80286, 80386, or 80486, you can better plan the time delays required in graphics motions.

I remember back in the first days of the 80286, when programs had been written specifically based on the speed of the 8086/8088 processors. Many programs, especially games, could not be run at 12 MHz—they were simply too fast! You may recall some of the Space Invader-type games that were so fast that computer manufacturers added a Turbo switch on the front of their computers.

this

wasn't really a Turbo switch, it was a "slow down so I can get the stupid game running at a speed where I can score some points" mode. Almost all the computers had a 6 or 8 MHz speed, while the Turbo mode might go up to (in recent days) 33 MHz.

I always wondered why someone would want to buy a state-of-the-art PC, running at 50 MHz, and ask for the ability to slow the machine down to 8 MHz. Was that for the days when they were too far ahead on a project, and had to spend more time waiting for the computer? Or was it for people who were paid on an hourly basis—they would do their paid work at 8 MHz, and their personal work could be done at 50 MHz, during their short breaks? Anyway, baffle them all and write your next game program to run the same on any CPU! That'll really mess them up.

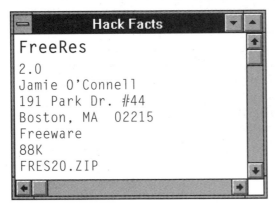

```
Hack Facts

FreeRes

2.0
Jamie O'Connell
191 Park Dr. #44
Boston, MA  02215
Freeware
88K
FRES20.ZIP
```

FreeRes is a small Windows program that sits in a small space on your Windows desktop and displays a lot of interesting and useful information. The date and time are continuously updated in the title bar of the window. The Windows mode, free memory, free resources, and free disk space on a selected drive take turns being displayed within the window itself. You can define the amount of time each item is displayed, choose what type of resources will be displayed, and select the disk drive that will be checked.

This program is useful for several reasons. First, all the source is included, so FreeRes is a great tutorial in C source code. You can learn a lot about how to access the information about Windows resources from reading the source code. Not only does FreeRes read Windows resources, it creates and uses a menu, manipulates a configuration dialog, and manages entries in the WIN.INI file.

FreeRes also regularly performs some useful functions. Since the time and date are displayed, you don't need to use the CLOCK program all the time. If you are doing development, you will enjoy the ability to watch memory and disk resources if they get low. I've seen programs that log data to disk die because the drive filled up. With FreeRes, you can see when this is about to happen, and perhaps do something about it.

Get your facts first...then you can distort 'em as much as you please.
—Mark Twain

In addition, FreeRes determines if you are able to play multimedia sound files. If so, and if you select the correct configuration option, it will chime the hour and half hour with a Big Ben-like sound. The first time, it might surprise you, but it's a good way to stay aware that time is actually passing; the half hours are a single chime, while the hours chime the appropriate number of times (ten times at 10:00, three times at 3:00, and so on).

Working with Memory

One of the biggest worries that programmers have had about personal computers has been the lack of memory available. In Windows, this is somewhat alleviated through the use of virtual memory. But since the problem still exists, there are a couple of programs that might interest you.

StackCheck is not a complete program. Rather, it is one person's demonstration of a way to add automatic stack usage tracking to a Windows application. The theory is that you mark the stack when your program starts, and then regularly check its status. In this way, you can see how much memory you might be using.

The example is not meant to be compiled and used without change. The author of StackCheck provides a small demonstration program, with a minimal WinMain routine. Then, two routines are defined. **dbgMarkStack( )** sets up some memory variables, and readies the stack to be viewed as needed. The stack is then filled with a known sequence of characters. Later, the **dbgCheckStack( )** function is called to determine how much of the stack has been used. This becomes very simple; just look for the areas of the stack where the known pattern no longer exists.

Since StackCheck is not meant as a complete program, you will probably need to do a little work to make it perform the functions you want. But the base is there. The code, written in C, is not too long, and provides great insight into ideas for the tracking of memory usage under Windows.

NewTrack, on the other hand, is a complete application that helps provide memory allocation tracking for C++ programs. It does this through replacing the **new** and **delete** functions in C++.

What NewTrack does, once it is installed, is to watch for memory problems. NewTrack was designed for use by Borland C++, but should work with other compilers as well.

NewTrack watches for overruns and underruns by overallocating space each time you call **new**. The extra space is placed on the two sides of the memory you are using. If these areas are written to, you know there is a problem in memory management within your program. In addition, NewTrack logs the address of the function that allocated the memory in the first place; then you can track who is gobbling up all that memory you thought you had.

To manage undeleted memory references (those where you used **new** and forgot to **delete**) and uninitialized data, NewTrack presets the values within each block when they are allocated and deallocated. In this way, it is much simpler to find out whether you are working with the right areas of memory, and whether you have correctly initialized them for your use.

When Is New New?

It is interesting to note the words people use in defining languages. In C++, the word new is used to allocate a new piece of memory. That makes sense. But why use delete to get rid of it? How about create and delete, or fresh and used, or new and old? Write your congressional representatives, and tell them that programming languages are getting out of hand. It will certainly give them something new to think about.

This may all seem like a lot of work, but it can go fairly smoothly once you are in practice. Using something like FreeRes (mentioned in the previous section) will show you that memory keeps decreasing during the execution of your program. After a day or two, the program may no longer work. Then you can call the NewTrack routines to try to track down the problems.

By the way, you don't have to track every memory allocation you do with NewTrack. You can disable the tracking for certain calls to **new**, and then turn it back on for other calls. This helps to narrow the problem, and saves time and memory in the long run.

4

Graphics Galore

Windows is a graphical operating system, right? How come everything is still text based? I know, you can probably add a picture to your Word document, and I know I could too. But where are all the pretty pictures, the line sketches, the special drawings that made books printed in the late 1800s so special?

I'm not sure what the answer to that question is. I guess there just aren't any clip-art books for old-time, hand-generated art that has been scanned into computers for permanence. So make do with what you have, and read about the next few items to help spice up your programs through the addition of some special graphical capabilities.

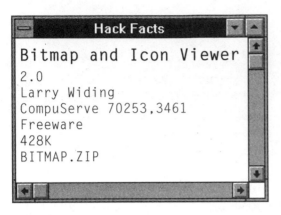

```
┌─────────────────────────────────────┐
│ ─      Hack Facts          ▼  ▲      │
├─────────────────────────────────┬───┤
│ Bitmap and Icon Viewer          │ ▲ │
│                                 │   │
│ 2.0                             │   │
│ Larry Widing                    │   │
│ CompuServe 70253,3461           │   │
│ Freeware                        │   │
│ 428K                            │   │
│ BITMAP.ZIP                      │   │
│                                 │ ▼ │
├───┬─────────────────────────┬───┴───┤
│ ◄ │                         │ ► │   │
└───┴─────────────────────────┴───────┘
```

The Bitmap and Icon Viewer is an excellent shareware entry. It's not the best program in the world (but then, no program is). But it is a very capable program for displaying and manipulating Windows BMP and icon files, and PCX and GIF graphics files.

This in itself makes the Bitmap and Icon Viewer a useful tool. I hate trying to pick a picture to add into a document without being able to look at it first. Did I want SHORE1, SHORE2, SHORE17B, or SHORE17A? With this viewer, I can take a quick look at each and then decide.

Even better, the Bitmap and Icon Viewer comes with source code! This means that you can learn about the import and display of several of the major graphics file formats used in the PC industry. In addition, since the viewer is a complete application, you can learn about the use of menus, dialog boxes, Windows Common Dialogs, and more.

In fact, it actually shows some new ways to use the Common Dialogs. The code was written in C and was expected to be compiled with the Borland C++ compiler (the Borland C++ DLL is used in the executable application). However, as I've mentioned before, Windows calls are Windows calls, so you should be able to learn a lot from this source code.

Learn C, See?

If you don't know C well enough to read example code, I would strongly suggest a brief overview course. Get someone to teach it to you. High schools and colleges teach one-semester courses, many companies teach one-week crash courses, and you can even get videos to train yourself. Or call me. But, since Windows is a C-based operating system, and has been from the start, not knowing C is like speaking English in France. Just because a lot of other people do, you think you can get away with it. However, you need to learn enough French to know that when someone points into the air and yells, "Duck!" that they don't just mean "Look at the pretty Eiffel Tower" (falling on your head).

Hack Facts

DIB and Print

Bob Rakoczy
CompuServe 100271,3155
Freeware
170K
DIBPRT.ZIP

DIB and Print is another graphics handler that comes with complete source code. This has even more usefulness, because it isn't just for graphics programs.

DIB and Print is an example program, written again in C, that takes the current window, prints it (remember the "PrintScreen" function back in the dinosaur days), and also returns a DIB (device independent bitmap) that can be used in your program, passed to another program (into a presentation, for instance), or stored for later use. The possibilities are endless.

Realize that a program is only a sum of its pieces. And this chapter is full of these little pieces. If you need them for your programs, they are here; you can save hours of work each time you use something that's already done. Shoot, sometimes it takes hours to find what you want in the manuals. And if you haven't done it before, an example is often the best teacher.

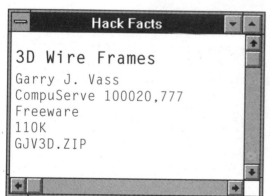

Hack Facts

3D Wire Frames

Garry J. Vass
CompuServe 100020,777
Freeware
110K
GJV3D.ZIP

Some of the best stuff in shareware is the documentation you get to read. Here is a note from Garry Vass, author of the 3D Wire Frames source code:

"This is a collection of classes (a school of classes? a herd of classes? perhaps a gaggle of classes? maybe a galaxy of objects? no wait—an Eintopf of Klassen). Anyway, this is an Eintopf of classes that I put together to do crude wire frame plots of three-dimensional functions. They are not efficient, they are not generic, they are not flexible, they are not great, they are not the product of inspired genius. They are simple, portable, and they work for me. I commented in some places and didn't comment in other places. Take it or leave it. Such is life in the download lane.

If at first you don't succeed, try, try, again. Then quit. There's no point being a damn fool about it.

—W. C. Fields

"Contrary to my fellow uploaders, if you find some improvement to be made, don't tell me about it. In all likelihood, I will never get around to fixing anything.

"You are free to reuse this code in commercial applications as long as you change all the variable names and claim to be the original author. If you give me credit, be sure to include a German translation so I can show it off to my friends."

If I didn't know better, I'd think that programmers could make some wonderful authors.

Anyway, this is a nice package for learning about 3-D wire frame graphics. And guess what? It's not just for C programmers! There is a sample program written in C for DOS use. But the Windows demo is written in Smalltalk/V Windows. At last, a non-C programmer goes public.

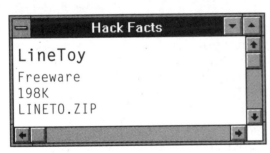

LineToy (shown in Figure 4-2), is another 3-D wire frame toy program. This one includes a full Windows application, ready to run, that displays three dimensional images (wire frames), and allows you to rotate, move, and size them using your mouse.

The program comes with source code (sorry, back to C again), along with about a dozen example images you can play with. The example files are simply lists of coordinates that are used in drawing the images. The program then lets you manipulate these images.

Using LineToy, you can therefore learn how to draw three-dimensional images in a Windows window, and then rotate them about an axis, change the magnification (how close they seem to be), and read the source code to see how it was actually done.

LineToy, like many freeware programs, was given to the public by someone we don't even know. No name was listed with the code or the documentation. We do know that it is someone who read a $50 book, found some Pascal source code, and converted it to C++. This is the game of life: BASIC begat Pascal, who begat C and his brother C++, who begat... Much of the shareware source code available today is in more than one language because people like you read about

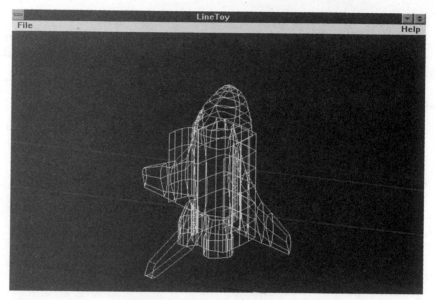

Figure 4-2. *LineToy includes a wonderful toy program for manipulating 3-D images in real time*

a package like this, and wanted it in another language. Once done, they simply gave it away for everyone else to use. It's like the traffic jams where you move backwards; each person you let into the line wants to let in someone else in repayment. What kind of repayment is that? You never get home for supper! But at least the thought was right; help other people when you can, and maybe they'll help you back with something you don't quite understand.

Enough philosophy. Let's talk about some source code with more zest.

The Fun Starts Here

Before you start reading this section, remember that you are a programmer. You write programs. You don't need other people to write programs for you. You don't care about what other people write. And you certainly don't need any fun in your life. The 36 hours you just spent finishing an almost-late package were quite enjoyable. I'm sorry the Diet Coke ran out of the machine at midnight, but that's the life of a programmer.

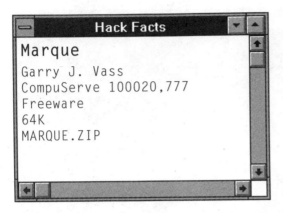

Hack Facts

Marque

Garry J. Vass
CompuServe 100020,777
Freeware
64K
MARQUE.ZIP

Here is a free program, with full source, that implements a marquee for your Windows applications. A marquee (see Figure 4-3) is a scrolling line of text, in this case located at the bottom of your window. As your program runs, you can put up advertisements for other packages you sell. Or better yet, sell local advertising time in your programs: "When in York, eat at Joe's" and the like. The more your programs were distributed, the more the advertisers would pay.

On a more serious note, a marquee can be used for messages that are used in debugging. They can be used for notification that new mail has arrived. These are the types of things that don't need to bother the user immediately, but they are readily available, whenever the user wants to look.

Here's another idea: how about a stock-tracking program with the stock prices scrolling across the bottom as they are received? Of course, you'd only show the stocks of interest, the ones the user selected at installation time. Perhaps you

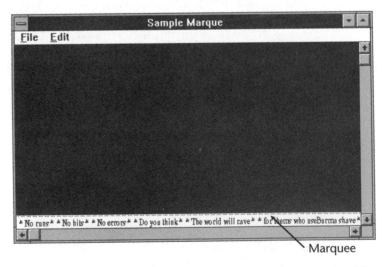

Figure 4-3. *Adding a marquee to your program can add great potential for advertising revenue*

could set limits on the prices of each stock, and display them in different colors if they go beyond those limits.

If you don't need a stock-tracking program, there are many other uses for the marquee. The source is in C++ and handles such things as the movement or resizing of windows apparently with no problems.

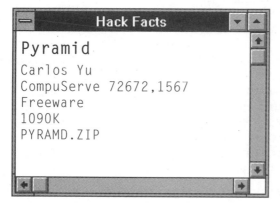

Hack Facts

```
Pyramid
Carlos Yu
CompuServe 72672,1567
Freeware
1090K
PYRAMD.ZIP
```

Here is a program that you will want to look at, inside and out. Pyramid (see Figure 4-4) is a freeware program that implements Pyramid Solitaire, a type of card game you can play by yourself. After long, hard nights in front of the keyboard, the solitaire that comes with Windows can get awfully boring. Hearts only runs under Windows for Workgroups, and then you need someone else to play (unless you're mad enough to take on the computer!). Pyramid is a good change of pace.

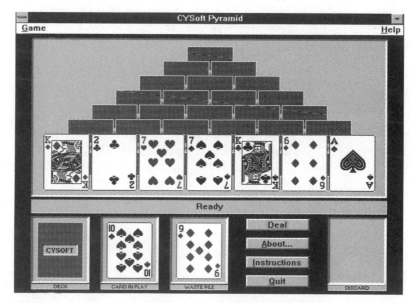

Figure 4-4. *Pyramid is a card game with complete source code!*

If you don't like the rules in Pyramid, change them. The complete source code for this game is included. Pyramid is great, not only as a game, but also as a learning experience for new Windows programmers. Think about it—this game uses nearly every user interface object available under normal Windows (we're not talking multimedia here).

i**f** you want to know how to use bitmap images for the card faces, look in the code. If you need to handle dialog boxes and menus, the source is there. If you want to use the Borland OWL (Object Windows Library) interface, this is a great place to start. This program was originally written as an attempt at an OWL program, or so says the author. I think that when you look at this program, both as an application and as an example of Windows OWL source code, you will be as impressed as I was. In addition, the fact that the code is free makes the whole experience even better.

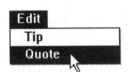

Where we cannot invent, we may at least improve.
—*Charles Caleb Colton*

By the way, it is interesting to note that the source code for this application is just a smidgen over 50K. That's not much source code for a full-featured game program. Some of this is due to the use of Borland's OWL code, which handles most of the Windows interface. Part of it is also due to the fact that there is a nearly half-megabyte resource file (containing card faces, and so on). Be that as it may, the main program is only about 50K. Is this the start of simplicity in programming? If Windows programming is not easy now, at least if it's shorter, it'll be easier in the long run.

o**f** course, as soon as you start playing the first game of Pyramid, your boss will walk in and think you've been goofing off all day. Just explain that you are studying some excellent Windows programming, and that you can even show the source code if required.

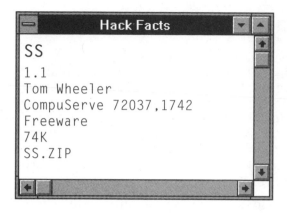

```
Hack Facts
SS
1.1
Tom Wheeler
CompuServe 72037,1742
Freeware
74K
SS.ZIP
```

While you're being marched off to the big office at the end of the hall, your new screen saver, built with the information gained from SS, will kick in. Hopefully, that won't get you into trouble, too!

Okay, you're back in the office, and you want to write a screen blanker that will put up an image of some really intricate source code, scrolling up and down at random intervals, so it looks like you're working really hard. Crack out the CD-ROM, and pull off a copy of SS.

SS is another of those programs written by someone who hadn't done it before, and once they figured it out, they wanted to share it with everyone else. I suppose it is a great feeling to give away something you've worked really hard for. But I know it feels even better to find a piece of code I can use—that someone else had to work really hard for.

SS is a screen saver program. It watches the clock, and when a specified period of time has passed, it blanks the screen and moves an icon around. If you press a key or mouse button, or move the mouse, you are returned to where you used to be (this is what Dorothy needed in *The Wizard of Oz*, I think).

How come wrong numbers are never busy?
  —Stephen Wright

What this screen saver does is not so spectacular as what you can make yours do. The shell provided here takes care of all the parts that you need to interface to Windows itself. The creative part is left to you.

4

Setup from the Start

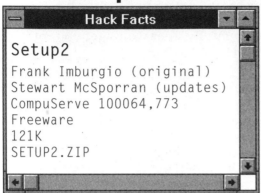

Setup2 is the first of several installation programs you'll learn about in this book. The rest of the programs are covered in Chapter 6, where we discuss programs to help you manage your business, because the better your program looks, even at the installation stage, the more business you are likely to find.

Besides, Setup2 is the only installation program supplied as source code. This program was originally found in the freeware market by Stewart McSporran, updated to present a more professional image, and then replaced into the freeware market. Like I said earlier, this program includes all the source code, so you can make any changes you want before using or releasing your own setup program.

There are a few things missing from Setup2, that you may want to add. For instance, it doesn't currently allow installation to multiple directories. You are only allowed one installation disk, too. These are minor limitations, since the code just needs to be in a loop to perform it for multiple disks.

you may also wish to add some sort of progress reporting (a bar graph, pie chart, countdown timer, or the like). But the current version of Setup2 is ready to use without any modifications. It even uses the Microsoft compression routines, expanding any files on your floppy that are compressed.

You will need Borland C++ to rebuild the program without making changes, as it currently uses some of the Borland Custom Controls. You can tell by looking at the simple screens it uses, as shown in Figure 4-5.

All the decision making is based on the SETUP.INI file. Here is an example INI file:

Figure 4-5. *Setup2 uses simple interface screens, but can be*
modified with the source that comes with it for free

```
[Application]
SizeNeeded  =2000000
Name        =Test Application
DefaultPath =C:\TESTAPP
GroupName   =Test Group

[Items]
;Filename,Description,[IconFile][Icon #]
;No Commas allowed in description!
;Iconfile and icon # are optional, but for icon #
;to be used, file must be specified
Setup.exe=Test App

[FILES]
;Filename=Description,Compress,Allow over-writing
;note: no commas allowed in description string!
Setup.exe=Main Program,N,Y
Setup.ico=Icon,N,Y
```

this file is simple and fairly straightforward.
Remember, you can change the source to handle
the INI file in any way you please. Currently,
though, Setup2 installs your application into a specific

I like work; it fascinates me: I can sit and look at it for hours.
—Jerome K. Jerome

group, checks for available disk requirements, and even allows you to select the icon that will be used in the Program Manager.

Do me a favor. When you are ready to release a package, include a copy of EZ-Setup (we discussed it in Chapter 2). That's the program that automatically tries to start a SETUP or INSTALL program from either floppy drive. In this way, your user doesn't have to worry about the drive and directory to use, the name of the program, and all that.

Higher Education

In this final section of the chapter, you get to learn about some other aspects of Windows that are most different from DOS or Unix programming. These pieces of source code provide excellent examples that can be used as they are, or expanded or included in your own applications.

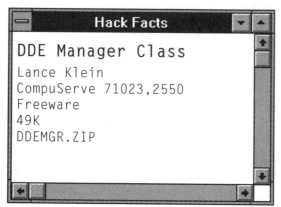

There are two files from Lance Klein included, both of which have some connection with management of DDE (dynamic data exchange). Each has a different purpose behind its use.

The first package is a DDE Manager class, written for C++. This package implements a full range of functions that allow the creation of both clients and servers for DDE. The *client* is the end you will usually need to use, as there are many *servers* already available (Excel, 1-2-3 for Windows, Paradox for Windows, Ami Pro, WordPerfect for Windows, and many more). Now you can directly ask these other programs for information you may need.

Using the DDE Manager class, you can make a single request for information, or carry on a full-fledged conversation, using bidirectional communications. There are examples for all these capabilities (single request client, multirequest client, and server).

In addition, there is a thorough discussion of the steps you need to actually implement a DDE connection. Be sure to read the header files (*.H) for this introduction to DDE control. This source code is supplied in C++.

Hack Facts

Program Manager/DDE Classes

Lance Klein
CompuServe 71023,2550
Freeware
29K
PROGMA.ZIP

The Program Manager package includes another version of the DDE manager classes, as needed for use with the Program Manager class. The Program Manager class is used to get information from the Windows Program Manager.

This class is used to retrieve the groups that exist in the Program Manager, and the items that are included in each of these groups. This is only available from the Program Manager using DDE calls, which is why the DDE class library is also included in the package.

Why would you want to know the groups and group items that Program Manager is tracking? For one thing, it gives you all the information you need to create an alternative front-end for the Program Manager. You could implement a set of pull-down menus, for your users not used to the Windows environment; each item could then be selected from a menu, even without a mouse.

In addition, you may wish to determine the groups that are available when your program is being installed. In this way, your program can be placed into an existing group, rather than having to create a new group each time. And beyond that, you can see whether your program is already installed, and give the user an appropriate option.

Beyond this, the Program Manager class is built upon the DDE class. This is a good example of object-oriented programming in C++. There are a lot of things that can therefore be learned by reading through the code. In addition, non-C++ programmers can read the Windows functions that are used and apply them to their own programming.

4

Hack Facts

```
Windows Serial Port
Example
Freeware
3K
SERIAL.ZIP
```

You often need to work with the serial port on a computer. This is difficult under DOS, at least to do it without errors or lost information. Under Windows, the story is complicated further.

This source code, created by an unknown traveling programmer, passing between projects of great importance (or maybe a guy in a basement or attic somewhere), shows how the serial port is used from within a Windows program.

There isn't much included in this file; it is only a couple of thousand characters all together. But I'm sure you know that sometimes big things come in small packages. This is one of those great things, and this is certainly a small package.

Many of these small files contain very pertinent source code not easily found in the normal documentation, or hidden there for the right person to find. I have two suggestions that seem to work in our office. First, keep these files on disk, and printed, in a special binder. Put an index in the front, showing each file's name, purpose, date it was created (or found), and size. Then file the disk and listing in the binder. Now you have a place to find the examples when you need them.

the

second suggestion is to immediately place the code into a format you can use. If you are using a language different from the source, try to get a DLL, and create the needed **include** files or definitions. Store this in the same binder just described. Start using the code whenever you can, to test it out for stability and accuracy. In this way, you can built a library of inexpensive tools for use when you don't have time to look for them.

Here is one more tool before we go on.

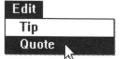

Edit
Tip
Quote

No problem is too big it can't be run away from.
          —Linus

Hack Facts

WDirList

1.0
Frank McCallister
1332 Magnolia Ave.
Rohnert Park, CA 94928
Freeware
114K
WDIRLI.ZIP

WDirList, shown in Figure 4-6, is another learning program. In this case, the programmer took the ideas he had learned from several others (through books, magazine articles, and other shareware, I assume), and put together a program to test his knowledge.

This program reads the current disk drive, building a tree of all the directories and subdirectories. It displays the total amount of the disk space used by each of the directories (added to the space used by all of its subdirectories). This is a fantastic way to find things to take off your system when disk space gets low.

I always hated looking for things to take off. Every time I did a directory, trying to find out the space in use, I was met with multiple subdirectories. Short of searching by hand, writing down all the sizes, and adding them together, there was little help available. This program fits the bill to a T. It

4

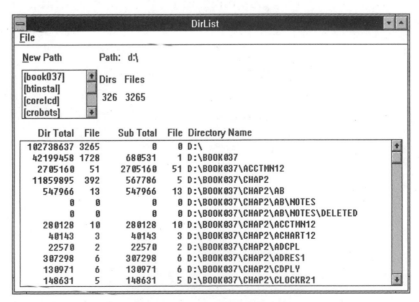

DirList

File

New Path   Path: d:\

[book037]   Dirs Files
[btinstal]
[corelcd]   326   3265
[crobots]

Dir Total	File	Sub Total	File	Directory Name
102738637	3265	0	0	D:\
42199458	1728	680531	1	D:\BOOK037
2705160	51	2705160	51	D:\BOOK037\ACCTMN12
11859895	392	567786	5	D:\BOOK037\CHAP2
547966	13	547966	13	D:\BOOK037\CHAP2\AB
0	0	0	0	D:\BOOK037\CHAP2\AB\NOTES
0	0	0	0	D:\BOOK037\CHAP2\AB\NOTES\DELETED
280128	10	280128	10	D:\BOOK037\CHAP2\ACCTMN12
40143	3	40143	3	D:\BOOK037\CHAP2\ACHART12
22570	2	22570	2	D:\BOOK037\CHAP2\ADCPL
307298	6	307298	6	D:\BOOK037\CHAP2\ADRES1
130971	6	130971	6	D:\BOOK037\CHAP2\CDPLY
148631	5	148631	5	D:\BOOK037\CHAP2\CLOCKR21

Figure 4-6. *WDirList shows all the size information about a disk that you would ever need*

doesn't hurt that source code is included (designed for use with the Borland C++ compiler and libraries). Imagine tying this program together with the Outline control we discussed in Chapter 3. Suddenly, you can look at any level of depth of the subdirectories, seeing immediately the size of all that falls below.

Hacking Ahead

Not only do these programs give you useful utilities, but they also provide source code, for learning and modifications. And without too much thought, ideas for even more software will come upon you. This is how great shareware starts.

I know, however, that as a great programmer, you have little time for much more than just programming. These chapters have given you a glimpse of the types of things available, and some ideas for where you might want to use them.

But if you do get a break, keep reading in Chapter 5. I'll introduce you to some time fillers that get your mind off programming, at least for a little while. In the long run, the break will do you good.

Programmer's Day Off

This will probably be the toughest chapter of this book for you to read. How can you take even a few minutes for a break from programming? What is a day off? If you're not sure of the answers to those questions, you need this chapter more than you think.

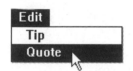

*Diplomacy is the
art of saying "Nice
Doggie!" till you can
find a rock.*

—Wynn Catlin

The trick is to figure out what diversions will be most interesting to the wide variety of programmers. Some people like shoot-em-up games, others like mental challenges. Other folks would just as soon spend time playing with their desktop setup in Windows, making sure all the sights, sounds, and layouts are just right.

I think you'll find something in shareware for any taste; this chapter will introduce some of that diversity.

Passing Time During a Break

I know, you never take a break. So this section is useless to you. I'll make a deal with you. Read this section, try out a few of the programs that are most appealing to you, and let me know if you can find time for a break in the future! I've broken these entries into Physical Games, which have to do with quick-thinking, quick-reaction games, and Mental Games, which deal with those programs that challenge the mind without requiring quick reflexes. There are also some programs that you can spend time with, without actually playing games. These I call the Non-Game Time Fillers.

Physical Games

Here we will discuss some games that are made for those who want to keep their fingers limber. Actually, you should consider these once in a while, even if you aren't much into fast-action games. I remember all the programming I did with only the keyboard. That was way back before the mouse came about. But it was not long before I quit using a pen; now, when I need to write something longhand, I find my hand getting tired quite quickly. Don't let this happen to your typing finger(s): beat the mouse—use your fingers on one of these games.

Quatra Command is probably one of the most exciting games for Windows I've seen. It uses high resolution, digital sound, and fast-paced action to provide a wonderful diversion. It is simply fun to play, and even fun to look at. This is such an enjoyable game that I've had people try to cut in on games I was playing.

Quatra Command is not a totally new concept; it is an advanced version of the original Space Invaders-type games, where bad guys come at you from the top of the screen (or anywhere, in Quatra Command), and you need to shoot them to get to the next level.

In this version of the game, there are dozens of enemy types that you can battle. Naturally, you can move around in any direction, you can turn your shields on, and you can fire at the enemy. Remember, though, that you can't shoot with the shields up; if you do, the shields immediately go away, leaving you vulnerable to enemy fire. Don't worry, you can get the shields back once you've finished firing.

There are even enemies who sneak up from the bottom and sides of the screen. Quatra Command runs in full-screen mode, leaving only the window title bar at the top of the screen to let you know you are still in Windows. It uses 256-color mode, if you have it available. This is about as exciting as the current crop gets and is quite comparable to anything you'll see on video games or arcades.

If you like your action fast paced, but with more intellectual stimulation, you should check out the next two games, both from Brett McDonald. In fact, for use during your breaks, these two games (Win Trek and Win Pelvis-n-Space) have 15-minute time limits in their unregistered versions. Time for a quick game and then back to work!

Do you remember playing the Star Trek game before Windows? I do. There were only a few commands, like move, fire a missile or phasers, short-range scan, long-range scan, and check the repair status. Remember, of course, that this game had to do with the original "Star Trek." And, it was written without any graphical capability.

Win Trek is a faithful upgrade to the original concept of the Star Trek game, where you run around the galaxy, killing the bad guys, docking with star bases, and racking up points. But with the capabilities of Windows, you can now get completely graphical views of

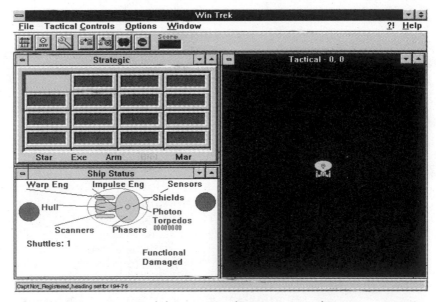

Figure 5-1. *Star Trek has come a long way into the next generation*

the short-range scan (like a visual view of the surrounding area), a long-range scan (minor detail about the areas in close proximity), and the current ship status (see an example of this new layout in Figure 5-1).

You now use the mouse to move around and make decisions. I'll bet that you could hook up the new voice systems (from Microsoft and others) and add realism by giving actual voice commands, if you really got into the game. Play in this one is continuous, so the enemies continue to move and shoot while you are deciding what to do. The older Star Trek games only allowed a single enemy move for each of yours, so you could control the pace of the game. Here, you either fight, flee, or die!

Why a Star Trek game? I've found that the "Star Trek" series is highly favored among many programmers. There is great disagreement over *which* "Star Trek" series is the best, but the concept itself is nearly universally accepted.

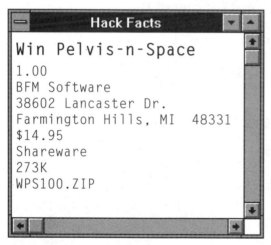

If, however, you are not a Trekker, you are in luck. Win Pelvis-n-Space comes to the rescue, in a manner of speaking. In this game, you are presented with nearly the same front-end design (shown in Figure 5-2), but the game deals with saving Pelvis, who isn't really dead. You see, he never died of little green pills, as some have reported.

Pelvis was actually kidnapped by little green guys who took him to a planet called Paceland, where they fell in love with his music. Your job, should you choose to accept it, is to find the planet Paceland, and rescue Pelvis from the green guys.

These two games are not the fastest action games you'll find, but they instead require a bit of mental exertion on your part. You can't just shoot everything and run. You have to watch your ammunition level, your damage reports (without a shield, you're a sitting duck), and what the enemies are doing at any given time. Using all this information, you can choose to fight one time and run the next, coming back later when your ship is in better shape.

If you prefer not to have the constant nag of a time clock, or an attacking enemy, try some of the mentally stimulating games in the next section.

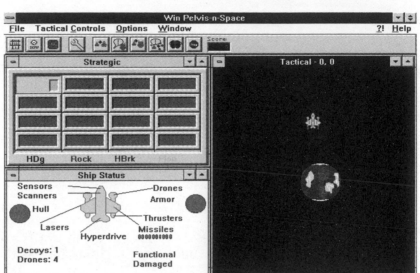

Figure 5-2. *Can you save Pelvis from the little green folk on Paceland?*

Mental Games

The games in this section are for those who need to wind down their mental state, not raise it to a fever pitch with a fast-action fight or escape sequence. These games give you the opportunity to stretch and exercise other parts of your brain, for something other than programming (yes, other mental stimuli do exist!).

This three-dimensional crossword puzzle provides some unique mental stimulation. You are given a portion of Cyberspace Virtual Real Estate, a lot that is 1,000 cyberspace linear units (CLUs) on a side. This means that you are in control of 1 *billion* cubic CLUs! I'll bet you've never even seen that many before.

So what does that mean, you ask yourself. Basically, if you look at Figure 5-3, you'll see what it means. This

The principal mark of genius is not perfection but originality, the opening of new frontiers.

—*Arthur Koestler*

game is a three-dimensional crossword puzzle that fits within your 1,000 by 1,000 by 1,000 cube. This means that theoretically, there could be 1 billion characters in your crossword puzzle. You would need to live forever to complete such a puzzle, but at least there's more to it than the standard Sunday paper crossword puzzle.

If you really like this program, you'll want to contact the Virtual Real Estate Division of Ivory Tower Software, and apply for a deed to your own billion cubic CLUs. If you want to sell your space in the future, have no fear. Ivory Tower allows deeds to be transferred for only $5.

So hop in your cyberspace cruiser and try solving these crosswords. It takes as much skill (or more) to maneuver as it does to solve the puzzle. If the words are too much trouble, but you enjoy the three-dimensional travel, try Amazeing! instead.

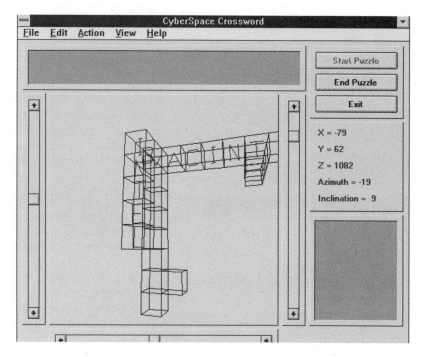

Figure 5-3.   *Quick, which way is the word going?*

Hack Facts

Amazeing!
3.21
Stuart Swain
Freeware
172K
AMAZE321.ZIP

Amazeing! (yes, the *e* belongs there; see the word *maze*?) is a three-dimensional maze program. You enter a maze and walk down the halls, turning and twisting as necessary to get out of the maze. Amazeing! has a lot of good options to make this as simple or as difficult as you wish.

A simple view can be used, where the outlines of the walls show clearly (see Figure 5-4). Use the arrows to move forward, backward, left, and right, until you find your way out.

Once you think you've got this maze thing worked out, move on to multiple levels! Yes, indeed, you can move up and down through the floors to 25 levels deep. Now, add color to the walls, and you feel like you're stuck somewhere where time no longer matters; you'll probably never get out anyway.

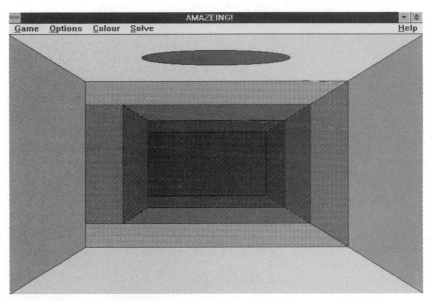

Figure 5-4. *Can you find your way out? Once you master a simple maze, move on to a 25 by 25 grid—on 25 different levels!*

Of course, there is a lot to be said for using mazes as relaxational therapy. I've seen several books that say you ought to let yourself get lost every now and then, just for the experience. Don't try to get out too fast, just walk around and enjoy the journey. After all, if you get out too quickly, you may have to go back to work.

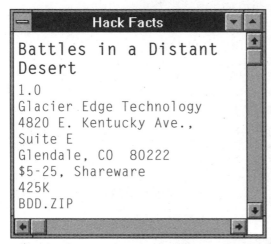

Battles in a Distant Desert, shown in Figure 5-5, takes you outside for your next mind game. Remember that little war in the desert not too many years ago? This game is a re-creation of the types of battles and skirmishes that occurred. Using a multiwindow playing field, you become the person in charge of the war.

The purpose of this game is to take back some things that the enemy took from you. When it comes down to it, I guess that's the purpose of many wars. Here, you take turns making moves, allowing the enemy to try something

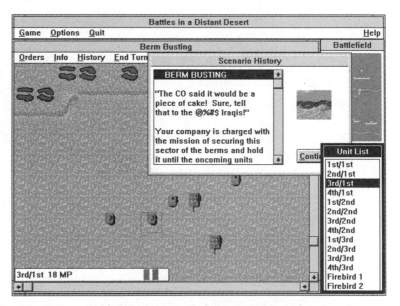

Figure 5-5.   *Take on the sand dunes and much more in Battles in a Distant Desert*

between each of your moves. Again, I guess this is the action-reaction you might expect from a real war.

You are in control of helicopters, tanks, berms, and all the associated parts of war. If you like war scenarios, this is not a bad game. There are a lot of possibilities you can try. In fact, you can play the coalition or the Iraqi team, letting you try your best at either side.

Luckily, when you tire of war, this game can be quickly turned off. Then, try the games in the rest of this section for some non-violent, non-three-dimensional, non-action-packed, intelligent interaction with your computer.

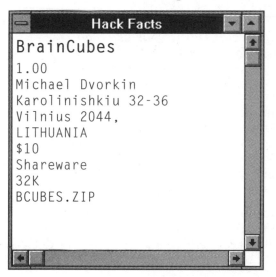

BrainCubes is one of those games you swear you would never be interested in, but which you end up playing much longer than you should. BrainCubes presents a very simple front end, shown in Figure 5-6, without hinting at the intelligence testing to follow.

This game is a replication of a simple test often used in intelligence testing and made popular by a child's toy. The game shows you the press of one button; you try to repeat the press. Then you are shown two presses (the first one, plus a new press). Try to repeat those. Then a third is added to the sequence, and you need to repeat all three. This keeps going until you make a mistake, or until you repeat the quantity required to jump to the next level.

The levels can't be any harder, right? After all, you are still just remembering a sequence of keypresses. Whether there are 4 cubes or 16, it is still just a sequence, right? Well, keep chanting "it's just a sequence, it's just a sequence" as you play this addictive game. The higher the level, the more buttons there are for each new press, so the game gets harder very quickly.

After a few times with BrainCubes, you'll find yourself saying, "I know I can get it this time, I know I can get it this time, I know I can get it this time..." This is how addiction grows.

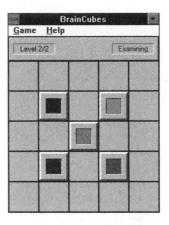

Figure 5-6. *This is your brain. This is your brain on BrainCubes. Get the picture?*

The next few games are for you card players out there. In high school, the programmers always got together and played cards at lunch. Of course, we were also the photographers for the school paper, and made up half of the track team. I'm not sure where the correlation lies, but I remember the programmers playing cards. Now, you can play all by yourself when everyone else goes to lunch.

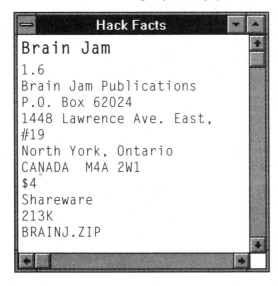

Hack Facts

Brain Jam
1.6
Brain Jam Publications
P.O. Box 62024
1448 Lawrence Ave. East,
#19
North York, Ontario
CANADA M4A 2W1
$4
Shareware
213K
BRAINJ.ZIP

Brain Jam is a very simple game to place, but it is not simple to win. It is a game of solitaire, in which all the cards are dealt face up, as shown in Figure 5-7.

The object is to move all the cards to the upper-left corner, one position for each suit of cards. The piles start with an ace at the bottom, and build up in sequence to the kings. Once you put a card on these piles (called the Build piles), the card cannot be moved.

Down in the ranks, you can place one card on another if the card underneath is of the same suit and one number higher. So, you can put the five of hearts on the six of hearts, but nowhere else—unless you want to store it

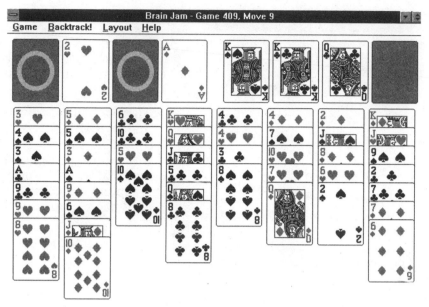

Figure 5-7. *All the cards start face up, so the game must be easy, right? Read on*

Edit

Tip

Quote

Football combines the worst elements of America: mass violence punctuated by committee meetings.

—Unknown

temporarily in a holding area (at the top right of the playing area). The four holding areas each holds only one card. You can move cards to and from the holding areas as you wish, as long as the card always goes on top of the correct base card (same suit, one number higher).

If you click on a card, the program will automatically move it to the correct position, if one is available. Otherwise, nothing happens. If more than one position is available, you choose where the card will travel using the SHIFT key.

You would think that this would be easy, starting with all the cards face up. And, it's true, you can form some terrific strategies in this way. But with only the four holding areas, and the rules for card stacking, there aren't always many options.

If this becomes frustrating (too easy, too hard, or too much thought involved), try the next game.

```
┌─────────────────────────────────────┐
│ ▬         Hack Facts          ▼ ▲    │
├─────────────────────────────────────┤
│ Concentration                      ▲ │
│ Solitaire                            │
│ 2.1                                  │
│ Stephen Murphy                       │
│ Pigeon Lakes Software Inc.           │
│ Box 13, Site 5, RR1                  │
│ Thorsby, Alberta                     │
│ CANADA  T0C 2C0                      │
│ $10                                  │
│ Shareware                            │
│ 504K                               ▼ │
│ CONCEN.ZIP                           │
│ ◄                               ►   │
└─────────────────────────────────────┘
```

Where Brain Jam starts with all the cards up, Concentration Solitaire starts with all the cards down. You play this one like Concentration, turning cards two at a time until you find a set that matches.

As you play, you need to remember where all the cards are (50 of them—that is, if you can), so that you can make the match once you see the card a second time. There is one rule that makes this simpler than a complete concentration game—you only need to match the color, not the suit.

Therefore, a queen of hearts matches a queen of diamonds. A black jack is a black jack. In addition, at the top center of the window are two cards that are "free." These are the leftovers, and are shown face up, so you can match them as soon as you turn over another match in the main 50-card area.

If you make an incorrect match, the cards return to their face-down positions, and you continue to play. The goal is to turn all the cards over in matching pairs in the least number of attempts. As card pairs match, they are whisked off the screen, leaving only the unpaired cards on the window.

This is a fun game. You can always win. Sometimes it might take more turns than you might like, but it is always conquerable. Now, how about a few games you almost never win!

```
┌─────────────────────────────────────┐
│ ▬         Hack Facts          ▼ ▲    │
├─────────────────────────────────────┤
│ WinJack                            ▲ │
│ 3.0h                                 │
│ Brett Liddicoet                      │
│ Opaque Software                      │
│ P.O. Box 2483                        │
│ Napa, CA  94558                      │
│ $12-19                               │
│ Shareware                            │
│ 972K                                 │
│ WJ3-0.ZIP                          ▼ │
│ ◄                               ►   │
└─────────────────────────────────────┘
```

WinJack, shown in Figure 5-8, is another game that's just fun. I enjoy it because it sounds good. Too bad they aren't making multimedia books yet, or I'd play the sounds for you right here. But they're not, so you'll have to take my word for it.

As you might guess, WinJack implements the game of blackjack, also known as 21. This is a card game that you play against the dealer. Your goal is to get as close to 21 as possible, without going over. Each

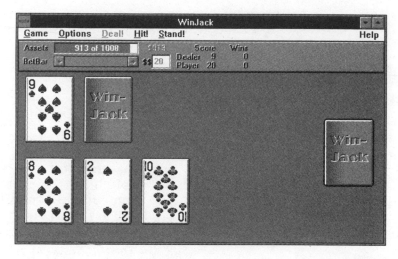

Figure 5-8. *WinJack sounds realistic. Hear your money going down the drain?*

card is worth the number printed on it. The face cards (jack, queen, and king) are worth 10 points each. The ace is worth either 1 or 11, your choice.

To start the game, you and the dealer are each dealt two cards. One of your cards is face down and one is face up (the same applies for the dealer). You can then ask to be hit (meaning you want another card), or you can stand (meaning you'll try to win with the cards you have). To make things interesting, you always bet on the hands you play.

Since you play against the dealer, whoever has the best score wins. If you go over 21, you are considered "busted," and the dealer wins. The same thing happens to the dealer; over 21 means the dealer loses. If there is a tie, the dealer must take another card to try to break the tie.

To make the game more realistic, and fun, WinJack uses cards that look slightly three-dimensional. They have added sound effects to nearly every function, so you can listen as the cards are shuffled and dealt. The setup options are handled using notebook-like tabs, like Quattro Pro for Windows and Excel 5.0 both use.

The package looks nice, runs nice, is easy to use (and lose), and not too expensive. In fact, the registration on this program is much less than you'd probably lose during the first hand at the blackjack table if you played for real! You might lose even more at DinoSlot, though!

Yes, it's a slot machine, another Jurassic nightmare! This one doesn't eat you in chunks, though, it just eats your lunch.

Actually, this is a cute game (see Figure 5-9). Maybe a little childish for a mature adult programmer, but it does spin like a real slot machine, and you can still have fun. Drop in a few of those stone coins, pull down the big wooden handle, and off they spin.

As the dinosaurs whiz by, you can hear the tumblers crunching. Didn't win this time? Try again. And if you run out of cash, you have two options.

First, you can change the rules for what constitutes winning spins. For instance, you can make it a jackpot any time a

Figure 5-9. *Dinosaurs they are a spinnin'*

tyrannosaurus shows up in the first position. Or make everything a winner of at least your initial investment.

Second, you can earn some extra cash by answering some dinosaur trivia questions. Sure, you're not interested now, but wait until you can rattle off those facts to your 10-year-old son; you'll be impressive, and you'll have a friend for a long time. Of course, once he finds out how you learned the facts, you may never see your computer again.

Let's try something that takes total use of the brain. Well, maybe not exactly total use, but total use of the 10% or so that we use. We're talking mathematical games now.

Magic is one of those games. Disguised as a simple game of dominoes, Magic is actually a mastermind of numerical wizardry. Or, maybe magic is what you need to win. The object is to pick a number and make all the rows and columns add up to that number. You don't really need to follow the strict rules of dominoes, where ends that meet have matching numbers, although that is an exciting level of challenge you may wish to add after you have won once or twice.

The display for Magic, shown in Figure 5-10, shows the numbers for each row and column, and their current values. This helps you determine the best domino piece to be added to each position on the board.

The pieces to the left, in the waiting area, have not been used. You are free to move dominoes from the board to the waiting area and back again. But you can't move them from one board position to another directly.

This is a good thinking-person's game. It's not simple to win and takes a bit of planning to even get close. If you like this type of mental stimulation, but aren't much into math, Pendulous may be a better bet.

Magic comes with both English and Spanish versions. Don't worry, the numbers are the same!

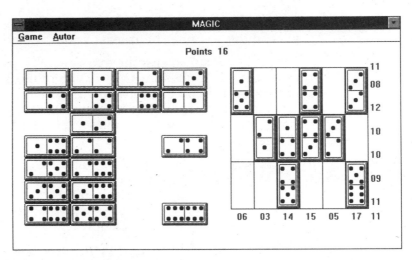

Figure 5-10. *Worse than a checkbook; can you make everything add up right?*

Pendulous is a strategy game similar to Stratego, but with a much greater number of options and capabilities. Here, as shown in Figure 5-11, you are a captain of the army and need to move your troops to take and retake portions of the country over which you battle.

The game is not too difficult to learn, and you can play against a friend or against the computer. In fact, to learn the game, it is suggested in the documentation that you watch two computer players battle for a time. I know I saw this on an episode of "Star Trek": two worlds battled via computer. When you were notified that you had died (in the simulation), you reported to a chamber where you would be killed. All we need to do is convince governments that they should work things out via computer simulation. Then, when someone loses, they can play a game of DinoSlot to determine the take of the winner. What a simple way to take care of the world's problems.

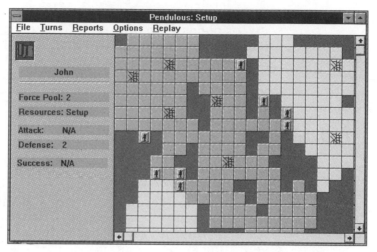

Figure 5-11. *Pendulous is a battlefield over which you strategize, planning the life and death of non-existent armies*

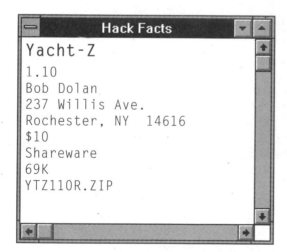

Yacht-Z is one more game of chance for you to try. This is based on the Yahtzee board game, in which you roll five dice, trying to make up certain hands of cards. For instance, you can form two, three, or four of a kind; a full house (three of one card, two of another); a short straight (four cards in a row); a long straight (all five cards in a row); or a Yahtzee (five of a kind).

In the computerized version of this game, you roll the dice and play three games at one time. You try to match a list of different poker hands (two-of-a-kind, three-of-a-kind, four-of-a-kind, full-house, short straight, long straight, etc.), getting the best hands that you can out of each roll. For instance, if you rolled a 2, 3, 4, 4, and 4, you could use it as your three-of-a-kind entry, as two-of-a-kind, or put it in your score for 4's (that's not a poker hand, but you try to get the highest number of each digit as another set of hands).

After your first roll, you can roll twice more, changing all, any, or none of the dice each time. In this way, as in poker, you try to build your best "hand." This is another game that isn't too hard to learn on the surface, but there are a lot of rules and permutations for getting good scores, so it takes some work to get really good.

Non-Game Time Fillers

Sometimes you feel like a nut, and sometimes you feel like a game. But other times you just want to do something, aren't really interested in a game, and don't want to leave the computer. Well, the programs in this section can give you something to do, without worrying about scores, rules, or whether games are billed at a different rate on your time sheet.

Have you ever noticed that your mind and body work in cycles? Guess what, so has the scientific community. In fact, they have discovered something called biorhythms, which is the study of these cycles in someone's life.

BioGraf is a program designed to show you, on any given day, where your cycles lie. There are four cycles that are graphed (shown in Figure 5-12): Physical, Emotional, Intellectual, and Intuitional. Based on your birthday, then, BioGraf shows you where each of the cycles falls for the current (or any other) day. In addition, BioGraf will actually give you an interpretation for a specific day. For instance, today my biorhythm reads: "Physically and emotionally you're in fine form at the moment. But with your intellectual and intuitional cycles in their passive phases, your thinking might well be a bit slower than normal, and your hunches may be few and far between." Guess I should have stayed home in bed!

The four cycles run during your entire life. Each of them is of a different length, and relates to different parts of your life, as shown in the table below.

Everything should be as simple as possible. But to do that you have to master complexity.
—Butler Lampson

CYCLE	DURATION	WHAT IT AFFECTS
Physical	23 days	Aspects relating to your physical body, such as strength, speed, stamina, resistance to disease, coordination, etc.
Emotional	28 days	Aspects relating to your emotional stability, moodiness, sensitivity, and even creativity
Intellectual	33 days	Aspects of your judgment and decision-making skills: mental alertness, logic, grasp of concepts, recall of items previously learned and the ability to learn more, and how well you can analyze situations
Intuitional	38 days	Aspects that are not fully defined scientifically, such as your sixth sense, instincts and hunches, and other unconscious perceptions. Even biorhythm followers don't always count on the validity of the intuitional cycle, but that is often because of the disbelief in items like the sixth sense, etc.

Biorhythms—the calculated horoscope for those of us with computers. No magic necessary, just a simple birth date. Does this all work? Many people believe so. My question is: does looking at your biorhythm make your day turn out that way, or does your day turn out the way it does because of how the cycles actually fell for the day? Another great cosmic mystery, I guess.

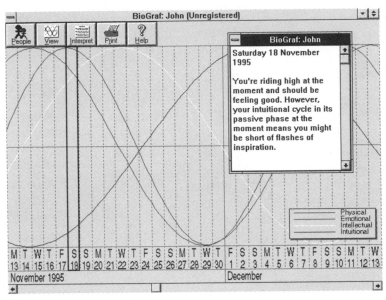

Figure 5-12. *Looks like it'll be a good day for something. To find out what, maybe you should consult your biorhythms*

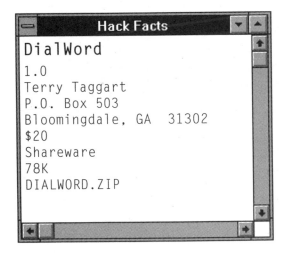

Hack Facts

DialWord
1.0
Terry Taggart
P.O. Box 503
Bloomingdale, GA 31302
$20
Shareware
78K
DIALWORD.ZIP

So let's move on to another time filler. DialWord is a little program for making up words from the letters that correspond to the numbers in telephone numbers. This can be very helpful, in that you can use the results to better remember phone numbers. For instance, 1-800-PICASSO would be much simpler to remember than 1-800-742-2776.

On the other hand, there aren't a lot of phone numbers that actually make up meaningful, informative words (see Figure 5-13). If there is a word to be made from your phone number, DialWord will help you find it.

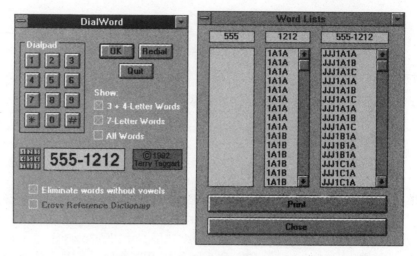

Figure 5-13.   *Here are all the words we get from the directory assistance phone number. Maybe it'll help you remember the number more easily*

Given your phone number, DialWord can look for three-letter words from your exchange, four-letter words from the second half of your number, or seven-letter words for the whole number. Or, you can look at all three batches at once.

This can be fun. Do any of your friends have numbers they should be repeating in public? Or shouldn't be? Luckily, when you want a certain word in your phone number, you can figure out what number would correspond to the letters of that word and then ask for that number. Otherwise, we'd never have phone numbers with reasonable names. Wait till we all have our own permanent phone numbers. Then, will we go by our names, social security numbers, driver's license numbers, or phone numbers? How will we ever remember which is which? I suppose asking for them all to be the same would be too much to expect ...Better write to your congressional rep again!

Sights and Sounds

So far in this chapter, I've shown you programs that you can use during your breaks from programming. In this section, we'll talk about some toys you can install for use *during* your programming sessions. These are the screen blankers, sounds, background bitmaps, icons, fonts, and mouse chasers (as I call them) that can be part of your work all the time (and the boss can't even complain—you're becoming more productive because of the mental stress relief provided by these shareware items).

Screen Savers and Blankers

With the introduction of Windows 3.1, Microsoft made it very simple for programmers to create and install their own screen-blanking utilities, also known as screen savers. In this section, I'll tell you about some of the great blankers that have resulted. Can you imagine being hired to write a screen blanker that basically advertises that someone is not working?

Screen Artists at Work

Screen blankers used to blank your screen. This was done to help prevent images from burning themselves permanently into your monitor. I remember a monitor at my old office that always had WordPerfect on it, even when you were running 1-2-3. That was burn-in. But guess what! The new monitors don't generally have that problem anymore. So think of your selection of screen blanker as more of an aesthetic choice, not born of necessity. Then you can have more fun with it.

By the way, these blankers are all installed through the Windows Control Panel, just like the ones that came with your copy of Windows. Simply copy the *.SCR files from the blanker you like to the Windows directory, and then select from the Control Panel. They aren't too big—take a few!

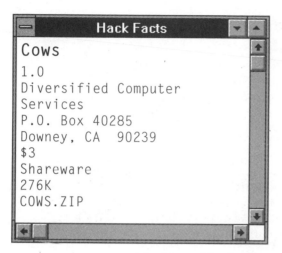

```
Hack Facts

Cows
1.0
Diversified Computer
Services
P.O. Box 40285
Downey, CA  90239
$3
Shareware
276K
COWS.ZIP
```

Cows is a fun screen blanker. It doesn't do a whole lot. A bunch of cows, and the occasional chicken, traverse your screen. You can pick the number of cows that are out and about, and the ferocity with which they cross your screen. You can also decide whether the screen should be blanked before the cows start arriving.

After a short while, the screen blanks anyway (else, why call it a screen blanker?), and the cows continue to drop by. By the way, these are not silent cows, so be sure to turn your speakers up real loud. You'll leave your desk, and be halfway across the building, when all of a sudden your computer will start mooing.

This is an excellent choice for those who are interested in black-and-white cows. Yes, some people really are! I know of a computer company that decorates their computer boxes with big black spots, I assume to make them look like cows. I have friends who wear cow T-shirts and cow ties, and drink from cow mugs. So you see, it's not as uncommon as you might think.

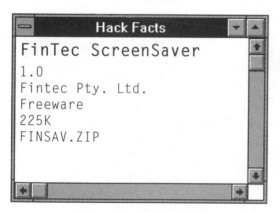

```
Hack Facts

FinTec ScreenSaver
1.0
Fintec Pty. Ltd.
Freeware
225K
FINSAV.ZIP
```

Of course, if you are not a fan of cows, there are alternatives. For years, people have been creating screen blankers that do one thing. Cows, for instance, only does cows (with an occasional chicken). They don't do clouds, or horses, or bumble bees.

The FinTec ScreenSaver doesn't do all these either, but it has a more random method of blanking your screen. It draws random shapes, using different colors and locations, to try to build up interesting pictures. These aren't pictures you'd want to hang on your wall (unless you are into cubic Picasso), but they can be eye-pleasing.

Blanker Pictures Have Been Blanked Out

I'd love to show you a picture of some of these screen blankers. The Cows and Kaleidoscope are especially fun. But every time I try to capture the screen, it stops blanking. Or it unblanks. Whatever you call it, I can't capture a screen blanker without making it go away. I guess you'll have to try these on your own.

And, they effectively blank your screen, keeping the colors changing to prevent any possibility of burn-in. There is no sound involved with this one, but if you're not around anyway, it shouldn't matter. Sometimes sound is disruptive; I've had screen-blanker noise totally derail a train of thought. After all, how can you program with a chicken or cow talking to you?

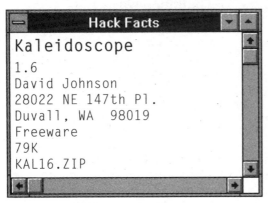

Kaleidoscope is one of the very best all-around screen blankers I've seen to date. It shows a whole host of designs. Some look like a kid's kaleidoscope, while others look more like a Spirograph. In fact, I've never seen such an array of setup options for a screen blanker. Look at Figure 5-14 for a glimpse at what I mean.

You'll notice a list of favorites along the right side of the panel. These are names given to groups of settings selected from the options to the left. Two of my favorites are Butterflies and Cosmic Clouds. But it is even more fun to pick the random selection.

Here you have an outstanding selection of actions that will cross your monitor. Some are more fun than others. The favorites are just there for you to preselect some settings. Once you find some settings you like, you can make up your own "favorite," and store it for later retrieval.

Kaleidoscope also makes use of high resolution, high color screens. The lines are drawn to look good on any system you use. And installation is simple; just copy the KALEID.SCR file to your Windows directory, run Control Panel, select the Desktop setup, and let Kaleidoscope be your blanker of choice. Then select Setup to personalize how it will run.

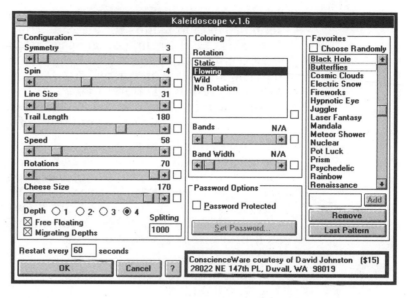

Figure 5-14. *A wide array of options for what your screen should do while you are away*

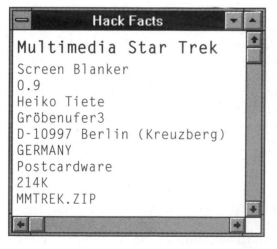

OK, back to Star Trek again. Here is a screen blanker especially for Trekkers. Multimedia Star Trek is a screen blanker that helps fulfill your need for "Star Trek" episodes when you are busy finishing a project late at night.

With Multimedia Star Trek, you can define a set of sounds that will be played at different times during the blanking process. You choose sounds for the start and end of the process, for when the ships are warping by, and for a period chime.

You will see several things happen when the blanker is running. Sometimes you will see Star Fleet insignia placed at different points on the screen. These are officer designations or small icon-size pictures of the space vehicles.

At other times, a majestic starship will slowly cross the screen. There are ships for all "Star Trek" fans: the original *Enterprise 1701* (from, you guessed it, the original show), the Excalibur class ships and *Enterprise 1701-B* (from the movies), and the *Enterprise 1701-D* (from "Star Trek: The Next Generation"). Different views of the ships are maintained, so you never know which way the next ship will be flying. Be careful not to step out in front of one!

Of course, this is enough for the diehards, but there is even more. Occasionally you will see an *Enterprise* (differing vintages again, but smaller views of each ship) warping across the screen. You can even select the warp speed that will be used for travel. These warp views are nicely done, with perspective held through the change in size of the ship as it progresses across the screen.

This is a nice blanker, because it does more than one thing. Our next entry is also multitalented, but departs from the Star Trek mold.

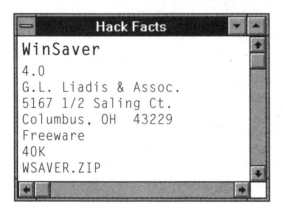

WinSaver lets you have variety without having to manage it manually. WinSaver uses a sequence of 14 screen savers, so you don't have to go back to the Control Panel every time you get sick of what is blanking your screen.

Not that you won't like a particular screen blanker (I can watch the Star Trek one all day, but then I never get anything done), but it is nice to have some variety. When using WinSaver, I saw first a group of lines that chased each other around the screen. This is similar to early DOS screen savers (I even wrote one similar to that), but isn't terribly exciting. But just be patient.

Soon, the blanking method changed. The screen was redrawn, and a slow scroll started. You know, like when the vertical hold goes out on your TV. The screen moves up slowly, wrapping back to the bottom of the screen as it goes. This is fun when you are talking with someone, and all of a sudden your screen image starts scrolling up off the screen. It's bound to get some double-takes!

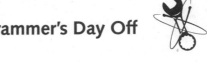

The computer is a very alluring machine, it always tempts you to do one more thing.
—Scott Kim

But that wasn't all. Before long, a new blanker kicked in and started taking pieces of my screen image and placing them at random spots all over the screen. "What's happening to your monitor?" At least when you press a key, or move the mouse, you can fix it all at once. Otherwise, you, yourself, might wonder what's going on!

This is a nice package for someone who

- Isn't into "Star Trek" (or needs a short break)
- Wants variety
- Wants something besides pretty drawings
- Doesn't want to have to keep changing the screen blanker in the Control Panel

If that person is you, be sure to try out WinSaver.

Mouse Chasers

Mouse chasers? Shouldn't this be more like mouse traps? No, this is a special category, for those of you who can't wait for a screen blanker to kick in (although you might wish you could actually sit back three minutes to see if you even have a blanker installed), but want fun things to happen on their screens anyway.

Hack Facts

BartEyes II
Randy Eccles
100 Ocean View Dr. #405
Dorchester, MA 02125
$5-10
Shareware
102K
BARTEYE2.ZIP

BartEyes II is a little program that runs as an icon in the image of Bart Simpson (another favorite of Trekker and non-Trekker programmers alike, and maybe even you!). As you move your mouse around the screen, Bart's eyes follow the mouse cursor.

Is there a reason for this? Maybe not, but I have found one good purpose. Occasionally, when you are working diligently, and set down the mouse, prying your fingers away for a small drink from the half-gallon cup of Diet Coke on your desk, you may not immediately see where the mouse cursor disappeared to. This is especially a problem on many of the laptop computers.

BartEyes gives you a quick indication of where the cursor is sitting. Follow Bart's eyes, and you'll probably find the mouse cursor.

Bart is also a welcome bit of comic relief when you really need it. If you put the mouse between his eyes, he goes cross-eyed (both eyes operate independently). Also, when you press the right button, his left eye closes (it is on your right, after all). And when you press the left button, his right eye closes. Both buttons, both eyes. I know it provides a few seconds of relief sometimes; I think about who had the time to write this program, why I like it, and whether I can show the kids without losing access to the computer for an extended period.

By the way, the source to BartEyes is available from the author of the program. This might be a nice example of managing icons, checking the status and location of the mouse, and such. Maybe you'll learn something from Bart after all.

Of course, all across America are people who do not like Bart Simpson, because of the things he represents, the way he acts, or because of his odd eyes and hair. That's OK, you can still get the advantages of a mouse chaser, without Bart's assistance.

Cat! and TopCat! are similar programs; a small cat chases your mouse around. Cat! provides a little kitten that chases around on your desktop, following the mouse in full animation. When the mouse stops, the cat sits down, licks its paws, and with a sufficient break, lies down for a nap.

Here is the cat you always wanted. It's cute, doesn't age, doesn't need to be fed, watered, or taken out, and stays on your desktop until you decide otherwise. The only problem with Cat! is that you can't see the kitty when it is behind an active window.

In that case, use TopCat! This program works in the same manner as Cat!, but the kitten stays in the top or active window. This can be annoying, unfortunately, since you know how cats are on paper! If you are working on a word processing document, the cat can really get in the way.

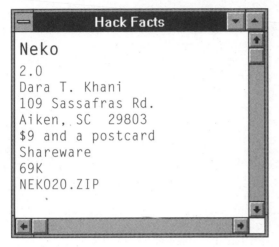

Neko is another cat you may be interested in. Neko is probably the best-known kitten on computer screens around the world. Neko does follow your cursor, but is somewhat different from Cat! and TopCat!

First, Neko is only a single program, and doesn't have to run as an icon. If it *is* iconized, then Neko the cat follows you all over the screen (well, actually it follows your mouse cursor, but you know what I mean). If you open the program in its own window, Neko stays in the window.

Also, while in the window, you can change the size of Neko from a small kitten to a normal cat and even up to a fat cat. This is kinda fun. Put a small window in the corner of your screen, and let the cat run around all day as you work. It won't get hidden under the other windows, and won't get in your way as you work.

What did I tell you? This is the ultimate pet. Plus, aren't cats meant to chase mice?

Bitmaps

What are bitmaps, you may ask. Actually, you probably won't if you are already a Windows programmer. The bitmaps I'm talking about here are the ones you use for your screen or desktop background—you know, the ones you select from the Control Panel during Desktop setup.

At least, that is the normal way to select bitmaps. If you use ZiPaper, you can have a different bitmap shown each time you run Windows. Not only that, you can keep them all ZIPped, saving lots and lots of disk space.

ZiPaper is a DOS program, so you will need to run it from your AUTOEXEC.BAT file, or from the startup command you use to get into Windows. But there are lots and lots of options, so hold on to your seat.

First, you can use either a ZIP (created with PKZIP) file or an LHA file (created with LHA). You can have ZiPaper select the bitmaps in the order they occur in the archive file, or pick them randomly. If you prefer, you can specify which bitmap to use each time (this option has a three-second time-out, so if you aren't around while your computer is booting, you won't hold up the process).

The first step in programming is imagining.
—Charles Simonyi

There is also a setup mode with ZiPaper that allows you to specify whether each of the bitmaps should be centered or tiled on the screen (Windows cannot figure this out on its own). You can also set up four different configurations (one for 640 by 480 mode, one for 1024 by 768, one for after hours, and so on), that can tile in one graphics mode and center in the other, or disable certain bitmaps during working hours, and so forth.

a11 in all, this is another great package for those who crave variety. You can use any archive file; just specify the right one on the command line. And with the various configuration options, you can enable the normal (read, "boring") bitmaps during the day (for example, the corporate logo), and then enable just the Star Trek bitmaps after hours.

Of course, having everything compressed means you can have even more choices available without using up all your valuable disk space. I've seen bitmaps larger than 500K! How many of those can you fit on a drive before you have to start cleaning?

I wanted to display a bunch of bitmaps for you in this section, but like screen blankers, they are not terrific for display in book format. Many of the ones included on the CD-ROM are higher resolution (VGA or better), with lots of colors, and they wouldn't look great in here. So I've listed a few of the better ones as follows and recommend that you install Paint Shop Pro (from Chapter 2) and start looking them over. When you have made your selections, ZIP them up together and use ZiPaper to pick them out for you.

And don't forget to register all this software. The only reason it's available is because of the goodness of someone's heart. But without any response from people like you, that goodness can be replaced with sadness, and the shareware market might just end.

FILENAME	DESCRIPTION
ENTD1.ZIP	*Enterprise* bitmap
FRACT6.ZIP	Bitmaps generated with FractInt (Fractals)
FRACT7.ZIP	More fractal bitmaps
FRACT8.ZIP	Even more fractal bitmaps
FRACT9.ZIP	Still more fractal bitmaps
GARFBMP.ZIP	Bitmap image of Garfield the cat
GLOBEBMP.ZIP	Full-color bitmap of the globe
JUPITER2.ZIP	Collage of Jupiter and the moon from *Voyager*
MERC1BMP.ZIP	Mercedes 560 SEL sedan (on your wish list?)
NATLBMP.ZIP	Assorted bitmaps of subjects from nature
NCC1701A.ZIP	Bitmap of original *Enterprise*
NCC1701D.ZIP	Bitmap of "Next Generation" *Enterprise*
PAISLEY.ZIP	Self-explanatory bitmap image
PARROT1.ZIP	Another bitmap—can you guess what of?
PERUBMP2.ZIP	Several bitmap pictures of Peru
RAYWINWP.ZIP	Ray-traced bitmap
REDPORSH.ZIP	Another wish list car bitmap
SHUTLE1S.ZIP	Bitmap of the space shuttle in orbit
WALLMAC.ZIP	Bitmap to make your PC look like a Mac
WALPAPR1.ZIP	Assorted bitmaps
WALPAPR2.ZIP	More assorted bitmaps
WALPAPR3.ZIP	Even more assorted bitmaps
WALPAPR4.ZIP	Still more assorted bitmaps

Take your pick, take your time. If you cannot decide which wallpaper you want, try them all using ZiPaper. But for goodness' sake, get rid of the Windows logo!

Sound Files

I am heartbroken. I hoped that when they designed this book, they would include a small set of speakers, and maybe a 5 watt amplifier. Then I could play some of the wonderful sound files that are available. But, alas, such is not yet the case, and you'll have to listen to them on your own.

Hack Facts

Whoop It Up!
3.0
Advanced Support Group Inc.
11900 Grant Pl.
Des Peres, MO 63131
$29.95
Shareware
147K
WHOOP.ZIP

Whoop It Up! is one package you need if you like to add sounds to your Windows environment. It allows you to assign sounds to all the things that happen under Windows. For instance, imagine hearing the swoosh from the original *Enterprise* each time you open a Window. When you make a mistake, the computer from "Deep Space Nine" can tell you that that procedure is not recommended. When you leave a program, you might hear "I'll be back!"

Whoop It Up! does all this and more. You can try out all the sounds, without even assigning them. This is a simple way to hear all those sound files you'll be getting.

When you start making sound assignments (meaning assignments of sound, not assignments that are well thought out and reasoned), you can assign noises to generic Windows events (for example, window open or application start or end), or you can assign them only for a specific application. If you are playing Win Trek (from earlier in this chapter), you certainly might want to add a few sounds for use during the game!

Sometimes you won't want sounds. Just turn off your speakers for a while. Sound files have many other uses, besides just notifying you of Windows events. If you are using FreeRes (from Chapter 2), you can have a Big Ben chime sound every hour and half hour. This is wonderful for tracking the time without constantly looking at your watch.

Game programs naturally are enhanced by the use of sounds. But you can use sounds in many applications. When you delete a file, should you get a warning sound? How about when you close an application without saving the files first? Sometimes a little note on the screen can get by you, and you get in the habit of saying Yes to each dialog box, just to save time. Would you think again if the dialog box growled at you, with the sounds of a large Doberman?

I hope that wouldn't cause you a heart attack. But do you get the idea here? Sounds are a part of our lives, and using them in programs is just starting to become reasonably easy to do (new hardware, better software, lower prices, and so forth). It's too bad I can't play some sounds for you here. But I have listed some files that contains lots and lots of sounds for you to look for on the CD-ROM. Try them and add some sparkle (or growl) to your environment.

FILENAME	DESCRIPTION
A.ZIP	WAV files starting with A
B.ZIP, C.ZIP, etc.	WAV files starting with B, C, etc. All letters are represented in their own file, except X
DS9.ZIP	Computer responses from "Star Trek: Deep Space Nine"
TREK_B.ZIP	Music from commercial breaks for "Star Trek: The Next Generation" and "Star Trek: Deep Space Nine"

Hacking Ahead

Now you have something to do, right? Well, don't tell your boss, or if you are a boss, don't tell everyone else.

Never mind, tell everyone. Each of us needs a break some time. When a computer is used as much as a programmer requires, it becomes a very personal part of our lives. Therefore, there needs to be some leeway given to workers for setting up their wallpaper, screen blankers, sound explosions, and all the other good things that make a computer a home.

The games are only for use during breaks. Remember that. Or write a book where it is your job to play games and pass the best ones on to others like yourself. In the next chapter, we'll be back to the office again.

5

in Chapter 6, you'll learn about programs that can help in the business part of your existence. You know, billing people, creating installation programs to sell more of your software, and the like. Then in Chapter 7, we'll talk about some of the really great information available in text files, online, and on the CD-ROM. I'll even tell you how to assign icons to the document files, so they look good in the Program Manager.

But first, play a game a little while. You'll be back to work soon enough.

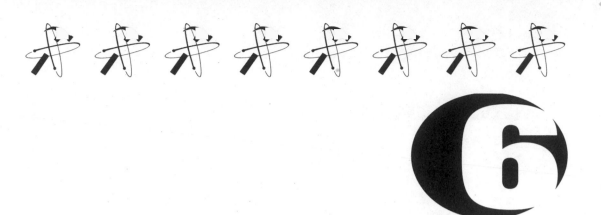

6

Business Manager

Throughout this book, you've been exposed to programs and files that can be useful in your everyday programming experiences. And in Chapter 5, you even found ways to have some fun with games and other diversions.

For many of you, however, this isn't enough. As programmers, you are very likely going to be in charge of at least some aspects of making money, or in other words, taking care of business.

Time Is Money

What you really sell as a programmer is the use of your mind. After all, they still haven't figured out how to make a computer program itself! And if they do, who is going to figure it out? A programmer, of course!

Other people may tell you what results they would like to accomplish, but the actual work of creating a program, that purely mental creation over which you have complete control, is all yours. Therefore, your time is extremely valuable, because each minute you program is something that can be used (OK, maybe it will need some work, but at least the pure knowledge has been developed).

Edit
Tip
Quote

Programming work is essentially unsupervisable because no one ever really knows what you're working on.
—Steve McConnell

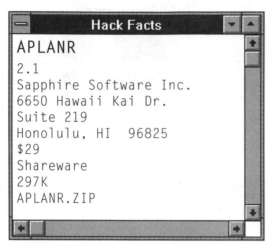

```
Hack Facts

APLANR
2.1
Sapphire Software Inc.
6650 Hawaii Kai Dr.
Suite 219
Honolulu, HI  96825
$29
Shareware
297K
APLANR.ZIP
```

If you are working on projects that have time schedules (as I'm sure some of you are), or working with a team on a project, you might want to look at a project planning tool, like APLANR. This is a scheduling tool, similar to many retail packages, that helps schedule the use of your valuable brain over a given period of time and pile of projects.

The overall project display is in the form of a Gantt chart (see Figure 6-1). This overall view looks somewhat like a spreadsheet, with small rectangles representing the tasks that need to be completed. If this was its only use, however, you'd be just as well off with a spreadsheet or a piece of grid paper and a pair of scissors.

Where APLANR really shines is in the information contained in each of the task bars. This includes duration information (how long the task will take or how many hours will be needed to complete it), dependencies (how the tasks fit together, which have to be completed before others can begin, and so on), and cost and income calculations.

If you don't know where you are going, you will probably end up somewhere else.
—Laurence J. Peter

In other words, you can start using APLANR as a "whiteboard," drawing in the tasks and dates that need to be tracked. This shows at a glance how busy you are likely to be. Then, as you want more detailed information, you can assign each task to a specific time period, and to the one or more resources (people) that will complete it.

Each of the resources has its own billing rate, and you can select the percentage of time that person will be available to work on the given task. So if Mary can only spend 50% of her time on a 40-hour task, it will take two calendar weeks to complete. If Bill can spend 100% of his time on the same task, it will finish in only five working days. And if both people are assigned to the task, it will complete in something around three days.

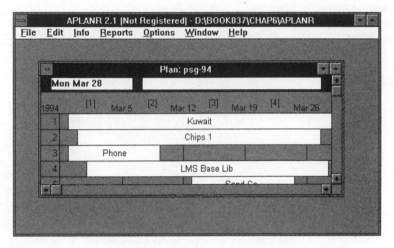

Figure 6-1. *APLANR shows and tracks project schedules*

By assigning resources and rates, you can quickly determine the income and expense involved with each task, and how it fits into the overall schedule for planning and budgetary considerations.

Heck, you can even use this program to schedule conference rooms, video games, or the VCR for lunch-time movie reviews.

About the only thing that APLANR doesn't do is track the actual time you spend on each portion of a project. To do this, let's move on to Time Log and Time & Billing.

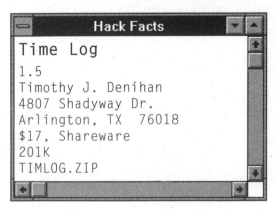

Time Log is a very simple program made for a single purpose: to track the time that you work against the projects or clients that will be paying you.

The setup screen for Time Log, as shown in Figure 6-2, is easy to understand. Just select the task you wish to work with, and you can begin changing time immediately.

Hack Facts

Time Log
1.5
Timothy J. Denihan
4807 Shadyway Dr.
Arlington, TX 76018
$17, Shareware
201K
TIMLOG.ZIP

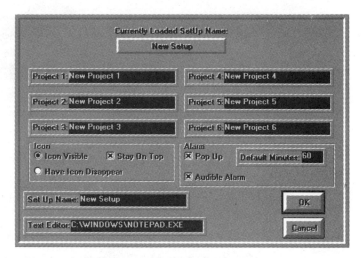

Figure 6-2.   *Time Log is a simple way to track the work that you do for specific projects*

This selection is simpler than you might expect. When you start using Time Log, you can give it the top six time demands that you want to track. These can be projects or tasks (for example, making phone calls, writing documentation, responding to user problems, and reading in the library).

you can also use Time Log as an efficient timer. It's very useful for those telephone support calls, where you'd really like to bill clients for all the time you've spent on the phone with them. Simply pop up Time Log when a call comes in, select the project the user is related to (or enter the user's name in the Other project), and an elapsed-time clock appears in the lower-right corner of your screen. This is especially handy when clients have paid for a specific amount of phone support time. Now you know exactly when to hang up or start charging for additional time.

By choosing your favorite editor in the setup screen, you can quickly view the current log, noting the times and duration of all the projects you've worked on (see Figure 6-3). Copy this into Excel (or another favorite spreadsheet), parse it into columns, and you've got all the detail you need to begin your monthly billing cycle.

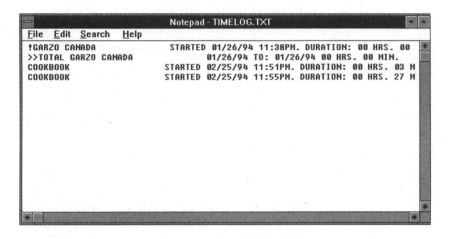

```
Notepad - TIMELOG.TXT
File  Edit  Search  Help
!GARZO CANADA              STARTED 01/26/94 11:38PM. DURATION: 00 HRS. 00
>>TOTAL GARZO CANADA               01/26/94 TO: 01/26/94 00 HRS. 00 MIN.
COOKBOOK                   STARTED 02/25/94 11:51PM. DURATION: 00 HRS. 03 M
COOKBOOK                   STARTED 02/25/94 11:55PM. DURATION: 00 HRS. 27 M
```

Figure 6-3. *With a tweak or two, you can bill clients for all that support you provide*

You now have all the time logged, totals determined for each of the projects or clients, and a way to create billing summaries with your spreadsheet or database. This still takes a bit of work, granted, but the hour or two you spend can greatly increase the income you generate with additional billings.

Hack Facts

Time & Billing

Leaning Birch Computer Consulting
255 Day's Ferry Rd.
Woolwich, ME 04579
$65
Shareware
413K
TMBL40.ZIP

If you want a more automated approach to the entire time collection and billing sequence, perhaps Time & Billing would be a better choice. This package collects the same data as Time Log, but provides a much wider array of capabilities. You need to spend more time learning how it all works, but you'll be surprised at how simply your billings are completed at the end of the month once you start conditioning yourself to the new process.

Where Time Log allowed you to track your time to a few different projects, Time & Billing allows you to track an unlimited number of projects. You can also track people (called "Time Keepers"), clients, and tasks. All of these have their own billing rates, too.

If standards are not formulated systematically at the top, they will be formulated haphazardly and impulsively in the field.
—John C. Biegler

When you start the clock, by adding a new "time card," you select the time keeper, client, task, and project. You can bill at a different rate for any of these items, or can bill at a flat rate. Having so many options to choose from can get a bit confusing, but Time & Billing actually works well and with little thought once you get used to it.

For instance, suppose you are a senior programmer. For consulting work, you charge $100 per hour. If you are doing design work, you charge $75 per hour. Simple programming is only $60 per hour. Other tasks may be even less, or possibly more. Using a rate per task allows you to better charge your clients for the specific types of work that you do. In addition, Time & Billing allows for a comment on each time card, so you can detail not just the type of work you are doing, but the specific task you are working on.

If you use fixed-price contracts, you will want to use the fixed-price charge option. Or, you may mark a specific time card as "Do not bill," so you can track the time without actually charging the client. Along with fixed-price projects, you may have a special rate for a client or project; perhaps the rate is a little lower than normal, to entice a new client to try your services. Or maybe the rate is a little higher than normal (you didn't really want the project, but figured you would do it if they were willing to pay big bucks).

after weeks and weeks of hard work, you finally bill your client. Assign all your time cards for a time period to the invoice number (maintained sequentially by the program, of course), and you can see where the detail came from, if you ever need to explain it all to your client.

Time & Billing does a lot more for you. It allows you to bill for the time you spend (don't forget, a mind is a terrible thing to waste, and even a worse thing to give away free!), track invoices for this time, and keep tabs on the payments received from your clients. If most of your billing is for your time, Time & Billing may be the ideal program for you.

Hack Facts

Financial Freedom
Billing Manager

M & R Technologies, Inc.
P.O. Box 061298
Palm Bay, FL
32906-1298
$35
Shareware
1.01MB
FFBMGR.ZIP

Edit
Tip
Quote

If you ever talk to a great programmer, you'll find he knows his tools like an artist knows his paintbrushes.
—Bill Gates

On the other hand, many people require more than just time billing. You may need to charge for hardware expenses, travel costs, software licenses, and consulting or programming time on a summary level. If this sounds like what you need, read on about Billing Manager.

Billing Manager is one of those programs I'm not sure about. There is nothing wrong with it, mind you. It just doesn't seem right under Windows. I mean, Windows was supposed to make all our applications work the same, to reduce training costs, ease the learning curve, and butter our bread on both sides.

But this program tries to be user-friendly, instead. It looks simple to use (see Figure 6-4); just press the right button and you start whatever process you need. But where are the menus, the dialog boxes, the CUA compliance?

Don't get me wrong. I'm all for originality. And this program does what it should. In fact, if I were a one-man shop, I wouldn't care in the least what the program looked like. But remember, we are all writing programs for Windows, the "standard." We use the user interface training guide and the common dialogs, you know. Where does someone get the approval to write a non-Windows-like Windows program? I guess I'm just worried that we'll end up like good old DOS again; each program with its own front end, none alike. That aside, let's talk about Billing Manager.

Billing Manager is written for us non-accountants who need to bill for our services (and hardware, and so forth) and track who has paid, who hasn't, who's late, and what our cash flow is expected to be. This is probably why it looks simpler than most Windows programs; it is meant to be as simple as possible.

6

You first need to put some items into the database. For instance, you must enter all your clients (else, how can you send them bills!). Enter their billing and shipping addresses, what terms you want to use for payment (Net 30, Net 10, Due on Delivery, and so on), and whether they are tax exempt or not.

What Is Tax Exempt?

Be careful when you are determining whether someone is tax exempt. In most states, this means that they must be reselling the items you sell to them. Basically, the state wants to get their money from one of you, but not both. What about services? In some states, services are taxable (software development, training, and so on), while in others they are not. Who pays the tax then? Your client, who needed your help, and purchased it, or their client, who actually receives the end product? I'm no accountant, so you'll need to ask your local expert. Just be sure you get the bottom line before you decide not to charge someone sales tax; it's really hard to go back later and tell them you forgot, and that they owe more money!

Billing Manager is written by an accountant, so all the right information is tracked for you to give your accountant. There is a complete audit trail of everything you do, but this happens in the background, without your assistance. The audit trail means that even when you delete a transaction or invoice, some record of it is kept, so there is always a way to find out what happened.

This program also tracks late payments and has a little note for you to send to delinquent accounts. It starts out as something like this: "Your account is seriously delinquent. In order for us to continue to deliver our products and services to you, we request that you clear up your delinquent account balance." Naturally, there is a way to edit this, but it's nice that the basis is there for you to handle all your billing needs without any other software or much other knowledge.

There's one other nice feature of Billing Manager. Once you have it installed, your company name and address are displayed prominently, as shown in Figure 6-4, and you get a

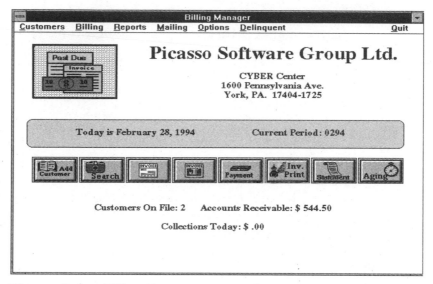

Figure 6-4.   *Billing Manager—a terrific accounts receivable package that doesn't even look like it's in Windows*

quick view of the number of clients you have, the outstanding accounts receivable (money you are owed), and what you should be expecting for collection today.

PhoneLog is one of those tools that you might have thought of making yourself, or maybe you do all of the functions manually. Either way, whether PhoneLog will be a great help to you or not depends on how close you are to the telephone billing cycle of your company. PhoneLog's purpose is to record all your phone calls, with the date and time of each call, the number you called, and a note where you can store the person or company that you called.

This is a simple way to get rid of all those little notes and pieces of paper that you might use now. At the end of the month (or really, at any time) you can get a report of the calls that were made. The version of PhoneLog provided with this book only allows the use of a single data file (the registered version provides a PhoneLog manager function to create new files, etc.).

Your name is placed on each record as your calls are logged. Your name is entered from an environment variable, so there is little work you need to do. If there are multiple users, you can quickly see who made which calls.

At the end of the month, you can check off the calls that were billed, and move on to the next month. Data entry is entered through a form, but you can scroll through the list of records in a spreadsheet-like format.

No, not everyone needs to track their phone calls. But if you do, PhoneLog will make the whole process much simpler.

All the programs discussed in this section have dealt with dates and time. They allocate, track, and bill for time. They determine when payments are due or need to be collected. Since all these tasks are based on time, you might consider using Windows Set Time to ensure accurate date and time settings.

Windows Set Time is a small program that calls Washington, DC, and requests the correct date and time from the US Naval Observatory. Version 4.5 of the program (available to registered users) calls the NIST in Boulder, Colorado, for such information. Your computer is then set accordingly. If you use this regularly, you shouldn't have a problem keeping your computer on track.

It doesn't take much to use this program. You need to know which time zone you are in, and that's about it. There are two EXE programs; one dials directly, and the other dials 9 first (for those office phone lines).

Every now and then, all you need to do is use Clocker (from Chapter 2) to set up a late-night call with Windows Set Time, and you can be assured that your computer clock will be accurate (barring occurrences like modem outage and phone-line problems).

Creating Your Own Setup Programs

Why is this section in the business chapter? There is a very good reason. What is the first thing someone sees when they use your program? It's not the beautiful graphs, the exciting training tutorial, the ingenious calculation methodology, or the hand-painted icons. It is the Installation program! Whether you use a batch file, or handwrite detailed instructions to perform each step, the work that is required to install your program is the first impression your user gets. Remember, first impressions are everything!

Installing the Installers

It's really interesting that several of the installation programs I tried had lots of problems being installed themselves. Remember what I said about first impressions? Those installation programs didn't make it into this book, needless to say. See what I mean about first impressions? The best program in the world is useless if you can't install it!

Therefore, for you to build your business, you will want a decent installation routine for your program. Take the extra time to make it good; people will remember if it *doesn't* work! I know that some of you will write your own installers, or use the tools that came with Visual Basic. But for the rest of you, let's look at some of the programs available in shareware.

6

```
┌─────────────────────────────────────┐
│ ▢        Hack Facts          ▼ ▲    │
├─────────────────────────────────────┤
│ Champion Install                  ▲ │
│ Mike McLoughlin                     │
│ Champion Software                   │
│ 58 Abbotsham Rd.                    │
│ Bideford, Devon                     │
│ EX39 3AP                            │
│ UNITED KINGDOM                      │
│ $30                                 │
│ Shareware                           │
│ 35K                                 │
│ INSTAL.ZIP                        ▼ │
├─────────────────────────────────────┤
│ ◄ ▒                             ► ▼ │
└─────────────────────────────────────┘
```

The first of our installers is the simplest, with the fewest features. It works, though; don't get me wrong. In fact, it does some things that the other installers won't do. You just have to do a bit more of the work for yourself. This program is called Champion Install.

Champion Install is a bit more limiting in its options for installation. For instance, the user will not be allowed to choose the destination directory, or to choose from a set of options (for instance, installing source files for your newest library or installing graphic demo files for your paint program).

On the other hand, since you must choose the destination for each file in the installation set, you can send files all over the users disk, if you so desire. This even includes sending DLL or VBX files into the WINDOWS directory. But since you can't let the user specify these directories, you might be playing with fire.

Champion Install is ideal for the corporate programmer, who writes utilities (or larger applications) and needs to install them the same for everyone. There is no need to ask the user for information that shouldn't change from PC to PC anyway, right? So Champion is an excellent choice in these cases. It's small, uses the Windows COMPRESS utility for compression (if you want), and can use as many disks as you require for installation.

As with most projects, the last two percent takes fifty percent of the time.

—*John Warnock*

To build a set of installation disks with Champion, simply copy the files you want the user to have, in compressed or uncompressed form, onto a set of disks, in any order you wish. Each disk gets a file called DISKID, which should just have something like "Disk 1" in it. Put the INSTALL.EXE file on your first floppy disk.

Then create a file called INSTALL.INF, which is a set of commands for INSTALL to use. There are only a handful of commands, so you won't need to learn much. You simply give a title for your installation screens, tell INSTALL when to change disks, and describe the files and program group(s) to be installed. It isn't much work at all; in a few minutes, your corporate utilities can be ready to place on the network for everyone to use, with a dummy-proof installation (no questions to answer incorrectly!).

Hack Facts

SLS Setup

1.0
Stephen Sama
4006 Berrywood Dr.
Seaford, NY 11783
$25
Shareware
165K
SLSSTP.ZIP

Another one of the simpler installers is SLS Setup. This installer works in a manner similar to Champion Install, but the directions for installation are kept in an INI file (SLSSETUP.INI). SLS Setup has a few more options. For instance, you can ask the user to specify the options that they might want installed, and inform them of the space that is required for each one of the components.

SLS Setup will also place items into the Program Manager for you, but it allows the user to choose whether to create a new program group. You can also delete existing icons from a group (for instance, to remove an old version of your program), and automatically update the WIN.INI and AUTOEXEC.BAT files (if the user so specifies, that is).

For a setup program you can completely customize, look at Setup2 in Chapter 4, which comes with complete source code.

At the end of the installation, you can also specify that certain programs should run. This is especially useful in displaying the README file.

SLS Setup is about a half-step above Champion Install in flexibility. The screens look a little better (see Figure 6-5). But your users still can't select the destination directory (they can, however, choose the disk drive, so at least they have some control over what is happening). And you can allow selection of optional files for installation, so there isn't much reason not to use a good installer like SLS Setup.

6

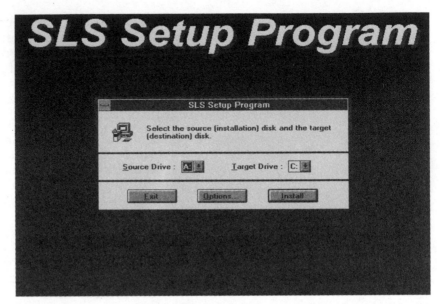

Figure 6-5.   *SLS Setup looks a lot like the better-known installation programs, but is available at a fraction of the cost*

Who's in Charge, Anyway?

I wonder who is in charge of my PC sometimes. Don't you hate it when an installation program assumes that even though you want a program installed on drive D, you don't mind piles of files being added to your Windows directory on drive C? I know, sometimes it has to be done that way, but I sure wish I had some say over what went where during an installation. Besides, my C drive is often fairly full with Windows virtual memory, temp files, network print spooler space, and such. I've even had installations fail halfway through when drive C filled up. What then? I didn't even know what files they put on drive C. Don't write software that way; let your users set things up the way they need to. They'll appreciate it!

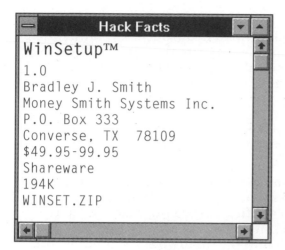

Now we move on to the more full-featured, and slightly more expensive installers. The first is WinSetup. This program makes life simpler for the programmer by removing some of the work in setting up your installation disks. You still need to copy the files to the floppy disks yourself, filling them in the best that you can (and need to create a SETUP.INF file to describe what WinSetup should do with each disk). But WinSetup comes with a dialog-driven front end (see Figure 6-6) to generate the INF files.

WinSetup adds a whole raft of features and capabilities beyond our two previous contenders. You can select a default installation path, but users can change it if they desire. You can select the method by which your documentation will be viewed. Very often this will be with the Windows Notepad or Write program, but you can be different if you want.

6

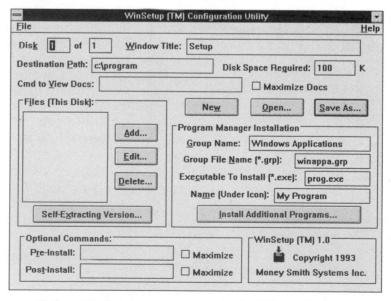

Figure 6-6. *WinSetup automates the building of your INF files. You still fill the disks yourself*

You can do multiple disk installations in a snap. You get to choose the files that will be installed from a list, rather than from the keyboard. You can designate the amount of disk space required for the installation, so that WinSetup can be sure there is room even before you start.

you can even run a program or two before and after the installation itself is processed. This gives you plenty of opportunities to communicate with the new user.

About the only problem I have with WinSetup (and it is definitely a personal bias, not a program flaw) is that there are only two ways to place files on the floppy disks—either uncompressed, or in a self-extracting archive file. This seems to throw a glitch into the otherwise smooth flow that WinSetup follows; now, I have to go out into another software package and create self-extracting EXE files for all of the disks.

I suppose no program is perfect (unless I write it for myself, and then, by the time I'm finished, what I wanted to do has changed, so I have to start over anyway), but WinSetup comes real close for a shareware installation tool.

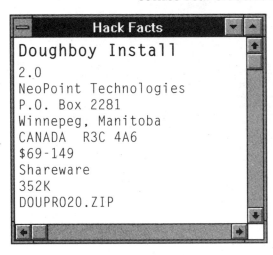

```
Hack Facts

Doughboy Install
2.0
NeoPoint Technologies
P.O. Box 2281
Winnepeg, Manitoba
CANADA  R3C 4A6
$69-149
Shareware
352K
DOUPRO20.ZIP
```

But there is one more entry in the installation wars that you should consider. Remember, each of these tools has a place in the programmer's tool chest, depending on the needs at a given time. The last entry is Doughboy Install; with features like these, you may not need to look any further for an installation tool:

- Data compression is built in. There is no need for any external tools, and no need to leave Doughboy to perform compressions.

- You don't need to write any INF or INI files.

- Doughboy Install uses CRC-32 data checking, to be sure that the files you put on the disk arrive on your end-user's computer in exactly the right form.

- Large files are split across multiple floppy disks automatically.

- The process of copying files to the floppy disks is handled by Doughboy. You don't need to prebuild any disks.

- You can use your own bitmapped logo as a backdrop for the installation process. This sure beats a blank or otherwise boring background. Free advertising, too!

All you have to do to get started with Doughboy Install is to create on your hard drive an image of what you wish to install on the end-user's system. This can include all the subdirectories you want, as long as they all come off a single base directory.

Once your own copy of the program is set up, run Doughboy, specify a few options (shown in Figure 6-7), such as the directory where the program is set up, the floppy disk to

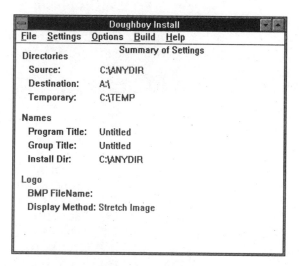

Figure 6-7. *Doughboy looks deceptively simple, but sports lots of options for building your own installation routines*

Only a mediocre man is always at his best.
—W. Somerset Maugham

which the installation should be written, the program title, the requested installation directory for the end-user, the group into which the program should be installed in the Program Manager, and any bitmap image file that you wish displayed during installation. The installation set of disks will be generated automatically.

Doughboy Install doesn't do installations into more than one directory tree, so you can't install those Windows directory files, unless you register and request the Professional version of Install. Then, you'll see a lot of extra features that help even more: system configuration checking, background color and pattern selections, installation of files into the Windows directory, selective file compression, and the option to start any program running after installation.

Help Me!

OK, after all that, you should be able to create an installation routine for almost any purpose you can imagine. You've written a program, prepared a way for it to be installed, and now you're finished, right? Well, not quite.

The next thing you need to do is create a useful help system for your users. This is one of the best methods for reducing the amount of support you need to provide. After all, if I can press a Help key at any time, and get help for what I am doing, I won't need to call you for help. Right?

The normal way an unenlightened person might create a help file would be to use a word processor that creates RTF (rich text format) files, which are required for creation of help files. The person would enter the help information, try to create different topics, and manually tie everything together through some sort of link scheme. Then he or she would exit to DOS and use the Help Compiler to actually convert the RTF file into an HLP file.

You, of course, are now an enlightened Windows programmer (else why be reading this book, and how did you get

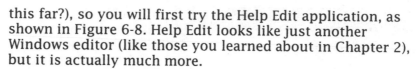

this far?), so you will first try the Help Edit application, as shown in Figure 6-8. Help Edit looks like just another Windows editor (like those you learned about in Chapter 2), but it is actually much more.

Help Edit can read-in ASCII text files and create RTF files for use in generating help files. Building links is simplified by means of a button bar at the top of the editing window. Buttons are available for creating new topics, definitions, and more.

Once you type in all your help text, define the necessary links, and feel that you are ready to generate a help file, Help Edit will actually call the help compiler for you, and then let you test the final help file, all without leaving the Help Edit application! Productivity can soar when all you need to remember is how to call Help Edit—everything else is taken care of for you.

By the way, Help Edit doesn't limit your creativity; your help files can include colors, bitmaps, fonts, and all the niceties we've come to expect from big-budget, professional software. But we've got everyone fooled. With Help Edit, the whole process is not as difficult as everyone thinks.

6

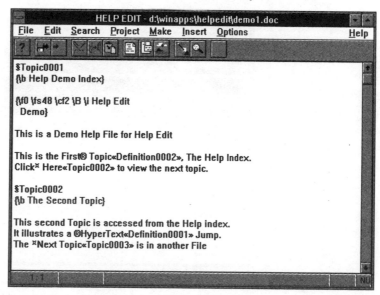

Figure 6-8. *Help Edit looks simple, but carries the power you need to produce professional-looking Windows help files*

```
Hack Facts

Visual Help

2.0
WinWare
P.O. Box 2923
Mission Viejo, CA  92690
$49
Shareware
961K
VH.ZIP
```

If you'd like to stay in an environment like Visual Basic or Visual C++ (or any of the other new graphical development environments), you may wish to look into Visual Help (original name, huh!). This environment looks like a Visual-something clone, as shown in Figure 6-9, and is about as simple to use.

Is there a reason to use Visual Help, when you already know about Help Edit? Sure, it's the same reason you wanted to use Help Edit rather than doing everything by hand. Visual Help is a very simple-to-use, easy-to-follow way to create help files. If you can, train everyone in your office to use it. Then, anyone can help you with help files.

Of course, help files are used for more than just program help these days. Several of the online magazines covered in Chapter 7 are distributed as Windows help files. With a tool

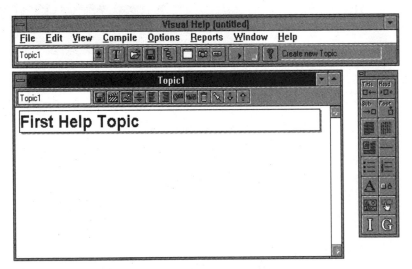

Figure 6-9. *Visual Help joins the other Visual environments to simplify the creation of Windows help files*

like Visual Help, you can quickly generate help files for all kinds of documentation, such as:

- Employee manuals

- Training guides

- Reference material for programmers in your office: for example, standards, procedures, and commonly used library reference information

- Newsletters for your clients, whether they are inside or outside your organization

Visual Help allows the use of colors, fonts, and bitmaps, naturally. It also allows the use of sound files. This is it—the ultimate newsletter that can read itself to you at the click of a button! This may sound like I am being facetious, but think of the applications in training! Teach your children to read! All they need to do is point to a word or picture, and have Mom or Dad say the word for them. What an exciting development for something as mundane as a help file!

Hack Facts

Print Screen Manager
1.0
Mallegrax Software
21446 Firwood St.
Lake Forest, CA 92630
$14.95
Shareware
260K
WPRTSCRN.ZIP

One last tool you may consider for building help files is the Print Screen Manager. As you are probably aware, when you press PRINT SCREEN in Windows, a copy of the current screen is pasted into the clipboard. From there, you can do whatever you want, as long as you first go into a program that can retrieve the image from the clipboard. No problem, as long as you aren't busy, aren't in a hurry for the image, and don't need to have a lot of options.

The Print Screen Manager can help a lot. When you press the PRINT SCREEN key, the Print Screen Manager intercepts the keystroke and brings up a simple dialog box, as shown in Figure 6-10.

Now you've got some real choices again. Sure, you can put that screen image on the clipboard. After all, maybe you

Figure 6-10. *Take control of your* PRINT SCREEN *key with the Print Screen Manager*

really needed to include it in an application that reads the clipboard.

But maybe you just wanted to print the screen, you know, kind of like the key was intended to do. In that case, click on the button with the printer on it. If you want to save the image, click on the disk button, and you'll be allowed to save the screen into a bitmap file.

When one doesn't know how to dance, he says the ground is wet.
—Malaysian Proverb

I find this last destination the most fun. What you need to do is create a bunch of screen images, each showing the hard work that you do. Open a bunch of windows (an editor, a debugger, maybe a help file generator like Visual Help or Help Edit, and whatever else looks like you are really working hard). Then press PRINT SCREEN, and save the image to a bitmap file, *in your Windows directory*. Now, change your bitmap to be one of these images. No matter what you are doing from then on, if anyone looks over your shoulder, you'll always look busy!

Hogging All the Resources

I know, I know, what is a Hog doing in here? This has a lot more to do with your software business than you might think.

```
Hack Facts

Hog
1.01
VacNat Software, Inc.
1003 S. Independence
Harrisonville, MO  64701
$20
Shareware
223K
HOG101.ZIP
```

Hog is a program that, under your control, of course, acts like it wants to use up all your Windows resources. Why is this important to your business? I'll tell you why.

I've been trying for years to get the biggest, baddest, coolest programming machine available to write my magic software. I'm sure you've probably done the same (try, I mean). Guess what, folks, not all our end users have gotten the biggest honkers either.

What Hog does, then, is allow you to test your application on a machine with less memory, less disk space, or otherwise limited resources. So, just as with a good installation program and a useful help file, you can better prepare for the support problems that might arise.

Hog is even good for testing installations. After all, use up your disk space, and the installation program should have troubles. Does it handle the problems gracefully? If not, look into another installer. What happens to your program when memory is about gone? Find out by using Hog to eat whatever memory might be currently available.

Do you feel better about Hog now? Another tool you can use, straight from the minds of shareware. Have you seen this type of tool from a retail source? Probably not. It's good that you got this book.

Online Services Revisited

A major part of many businesses is related to communications. Imagine trying to run a business today if we didn't have fax machines, telephones (cellular, cordless, and even cord-bound), and overnight mail. Where would you be if your only method of communication was by pony express? Business as we know it could not come close to existence without the modern explosion of communications methods.

In Chapter 1, I told you about some of the electronic methods of retrieving good software, like that included on the CD-ROM in this book. What I didn't stress, however, is that these same means are also quite good for communications. In this section, I'll tell you about some software that eases your entry into this grand, new world of electronic communications.

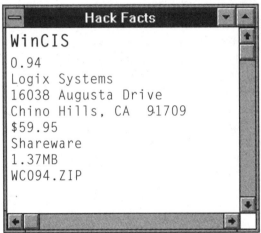

Throughout much of this book, I have spoken about CompuServe. Most of the programs in this book can be found on CompuServe, along with probably hundreds of thousands more.

But CompuServe is not just a large file repository. It is also one of the largest mail and communications networks in the world. With a local phone call, I can send and receive mail to nearly every portion of the globe. I can also send files, mail-grams, and much more. But wait, I don't want to become a commercial.

The WinCIS program allows you quick access to CompuServe, through a common Windows front end, as shown in Figure 6-11. This is a great help, because the CompuServe interface is, by default, text based, and rather slow and cumbersome.

Using a front-end program is not a new idea for electronic services. CompuServe sells their own front end (called, uniquely enough, WinCIM), which performs similarly to WinCIS. There are also front ends for DOS users, as well as Macintosh and other system users. And other services also have unique front ends; America Online, for instance, gives you their program free if you try their services.

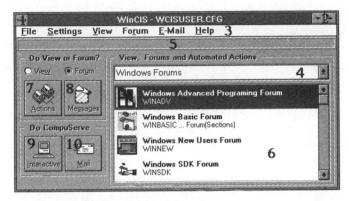

Figure 6-11. *WinCIS puts a pretty front end on CompuServe, the normally cumbersome (but extensive) electronic service*

What makes a front end nicer? First of all, it runs within Windows, which saves you a lot of time (you don't have to go back and forth into the DOS world). Second of all, you can automate much of the routine work you do with the service.

For instance, you can have WinCIS call CompuServe, download your latest mail, check a few favorite spots for new files to download, and leave a message for your client in some far-off land. All without touching the keyboard.

In addition, special interest group areas can be stored in WinCIS, so you can quickly move to favorite areas of CompuServe without remembering how to get there, or even what the name of each area might be.

Generally, front-end programs replicate the normal commands you would give were you logged directly into CompuServe. In some cases, however, they go beyond this normal duty. For instance, it is simple in a front end to mark a group of files as I browse around the file areas. Later I can download the whole set, logging off automatically when the download completes. This is nearly impossible from the text command line in CompuServe.

Everything should be made as simple as possible; but not simpler.

—*Albert Einstein*

Hack Facts

WinNET™ Mail

2.05
Computer Witchcraft, Inc.
Post Office Box 4189
Louisville, Ky 40204
Freeware
1.45MB
WNMAIL.ZIP

An even larger electronic system, one that is used all over the globe, is the Internet. It is a name you may have heard, but if you haven't, you will soon. As more and more people start to talk about an information superhighway, the Internet becomes more and more popular.

The Internet is a vast network of bulletin board systems and electronic services. By calling into your local (or nearby) node, you can gain access to thousands of Internet nodes with no further work.

WinNET Mail, as shown in Figure 6-12, is a unique set of tools for accessing the Internet. This is a great new type of software. Prior to this, about the only ways to access the Internet were either to be affiliated with a university with Internet access, or to install a full-time,

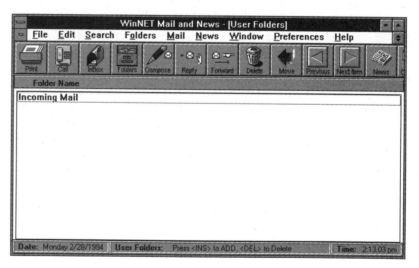

Figure 6-12. *Accessing the Internet is now as easy as running a Windows program*

See The Internet
Yellow Pages *by
Harley Hahn and
Rick Stout
(Osborne/McGraw-
Hill, 1994) for
listings of many of
the common
Internet nodes.*

dedicated phone line to provide anytime access from other nodes (and to pay a fee for access).

Now, companies are starting to install the Internet, and then to sell time on the connection. This is what has been done for WinNET Mail. The authors of the software are giving it away free, in hopes that you will connect to their 800-line BBS, with complete access to the Internet. Actually, you need to call in several times a day to be sure everything is picked up and delivered at sufficiently small intervals. How expensive is this? Not much different from the other online services.

Once you have access to the Internet, you can send mail to anyone who's anyone (like you will be now!). In fact, you will receive your own Internet mail address, so you can receive mail from anyone who's anyone. Start watching the computer magazines, if you haven't yet, and watch how many companies and people mention their Internet addresses.

The Internet from CompuServe

Did you know that you can reach the Internet from CompuServe, at least for mail access? If someone wants to send you mail, and your CompuServe address is 11111,2222, they would send it to the Internet address 11111.2222@compuserve.com. Notice that all you do is replace the comma in your CompuServe ID with a period, and tack on the generic @compuserve.com. To send mail back, address it to >INTERNET:person@his.address, where you fill in the correct Internet address after the colon. Don't forget the greater-than sign and the word INTERNET, or the mail won't be delivered correctly.

One other way to gain access is through a local bulletin board, one that supports the Internet connection. One of those packages is PowerBBS.

Hack Facts

PowerBBS

3.2
Russell Frey
35 Fox Ct.
Hicksville, NY 11801
$99-189
Shareware
3.2MB (installed)
PBBSW32A.ZIP
PBBSW32B.ZIP
PBBSW32C.ZIP

PowerBBS is a complete bulletin board system that you can run on your PC while you continue to develop, play, read, and write in Windows. What a concept! A program that allows people to call you at any time to leave messages, upload files, or retrieve messages and files that you or anyone else might have left for them, and all in the background while you continue your work!

This is one reason why PowerBBS is especially useful to you as a Windows programmer. You can provide support for your users without having to dedicate a separate PC to the task. You know, with a big development machine like you have, a few cycles here and there will hardly be missed.

PowerBBS also supports connection to the Internet, so you can provide a very valuable service to your users and others who may use your BBS. Charge a little for this service, and suddenly your BBS is self-sustaining.

There is a lot of flexibility and power in PowerBBS, too. There is a complete scripting language, so you can write your own rule for how the BBS should run. You can design your own menus and add any amount of security you desire. You can add external Doors (programs that perform other functions than are provided by the BBS program itself), run up to nine nodes on one PC, use the BBS on a LAN, and utilize special serial port boards for even better performance.

I don't want to sound like a commercial again, but if you want to consider a BBS on your Windows machine, look at PowerBBS, right here on your CD-ROM!

Hacking Ahead

You've finally got a hold on the software that is available for Window programmers like you. You haven't seen it all, but hopefully the taste you've received is enough to get you started in the search for the best.

in Chapter 7, I'll tell you about some of the non-program items available in shareware. These include text files, online magazines, and more. I'll also show you some ways to pretty up your Windows environment, adding icons to document files for a little spice.

Don't wait here! Keep going!

The difference between genius and stupidity is that genius has its limits.
—Anonymous

6

Document Library

Documentation. One of the last words that most programmers want to hear. As in, "where's the documentation?" Or, "did you write the documentation yet?" It seems odd that the people who need documentation the most like to produce it the least. I mean, can you imagine writing a Windows program without any documentation for reference? How would you ever figure out the message-passing conventions, Hungarian notation, and all the other many pieces of knowledge hidden within some document's pages?

Maybe the next question, then, is "why is there a section on documentation in a Windows programming book?" I'll tell you why. Because much of the information you need, if it is in a document you have, may be hard to find or utilize. The items in this chapter, all included on the CD-ROM, provide a lot more information about the tools you might be using. And since it is for Windows programmers, I'll tell you about some interesting ways of accessing and organizing these documents.

The Shareware Bookstore

There are a lot of files available all over the place that deal with Windows programming. In fact, not just Windows programming, but programming for DOS, Windows, OS/2, Windows NT, Macintosh System 7, Digital VMS, Unix, Unix-like operating systems, Motif, XWindow systems, and much, much more.

Plus, programming has no lock on the market; there are files available for nearly any interest you may have. But I'm being selfish for now, because this book is for Windows programmers like you.

Reading legal mush can turn your brain to guacamole!
—Amiga ROM Kernel Manual

Many of the big text files that are available are virtually books, in that they are large volumes of information, just waiting to be printed. Several vendors even put complete manuals out in PostScript format, meaning that with the right printer, your document will look as good as the original book. Yours, however, can be placed into a loose-leaf binder, rather than being a bound book (and not staying open when you are reading, especially late at night or when you're really busy).

There is a great variety of formatting used with documentation files found on the electronic networks and CD-ROMs. As you produce your own programs, help, and documentation, think back to which of these documents is easiest to read. Probably, it will be the one most difficult to print. You cannot really win, but if you expect your users to spend more time on the computer than off of it, make the documents interactive and computer-based. Otherwise, drop back into the printed image, and just do your best.

One of the largest, most useful pieces of information available in the Windows test file world is the Visual Basic Knowledge Base, which Microsoft makes available on CompuServe (among other places). This huge archive has over 600 articles, ranging in topics from bug reports and work-arounds, to almost any other topic a Visual Basic programmer could want.

As proof, the Tips & Techniques help file has the following table of contents:

- VB Programming Using Standard Controls
- VB Programming Using Custom & Third-Party Controls
- Optimization, Memory Management, & General VB Programming

- Advanced VB Programming—Networks, APIs, DLLs, Graphics

- Data Access & VB Database Programming

- VB Design Environment

- Running VB Applications

- General VB References & Documentation Corrections

- VB Setup, Installation, CDK, Help Compiler, DDE, & OLE

This may not seem like a lot of information, until you realize that each of these topics contains many entries (see Figure 7-1), so the amount of information available is staggering!

The list of topics in the Bugs help file is simpler: Unfixed Bugs, Fixed Bugs, and Updates Available. Each of these topics has pages of entries, though. All in all, there is a great deal to read here! And realize that not everything is only for Visual Basic programmers. I'm sure the bugs are specific, but much of the Tips file is pertinent to programmers in any Windows language. After all, everyone still calls the Windows

7

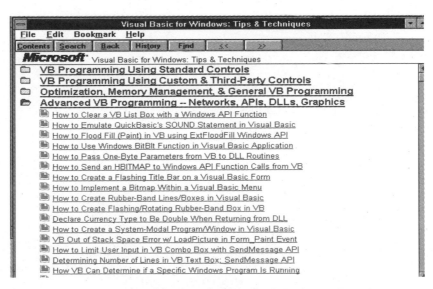

Figure 7-1. *Microsoft's Visual Basic for Windows: Tips & Techniques has hundreds of articles to choose from*

API and tries to perform certain functions, no matter what language they might be using.

This isn't the only help file of this type available, or even the only one for Visual Basic. In fact, VB Tips & Tricks is a non-Microsoft endeavor, where all kinds of good information are kept. Not only does VB Tips talk about Visual Basic for Windows, it also has a section on Visual Basic for DOS, and another section on creating Windows Help files!

The list of topics for Windows is shorter that the Microsoft file, but just as impressive (considering there aren't hundreds of programmers feeding the information mill):

- Buttons & Image Control
- Controls
- Form_Load ( ) Events
- Graphics
- Hot Spots
- List Boxes
- Menus
- Miscellaneous
- Text Boxes
- Tool Boxes
- Windows

The nice thing about standards is that there are so many of them to choose from.

—IBM

Each of these areas is further broken down into individual articles, detailing some small but interesting aspect of Windows programming with Visual Basic. There is a lot to be learned here, and (sorry to say it) this is simpler to read and understand than the Microsoft manuals, or even Microsoft's VB Tips & Techniques and Bugs files mentioned above.

```
┌─────────────────────────────────┐
│ ─     Hack Facts      ▼  ▲      │
├─────────────────────────────────┤
│ Index for Data Access        ▲  │
│ Guide for Visual Basic          │
│ Professional 3.0                │
│ Professional Features           │
│ Book 2                          │
│ Freeware                        │
│ 69K                             │
│ DATIDX.EXE                      │
│                              ▼  │
├─────────────────────────────────┤
│ ◄ │                         │►  │
└─────────────────────────────────┘
```

As a matter of fact, there are even files out there that hope to improve directly upon the Microsoft documentation. One such file is the Index for the Data Access Guide, found in the second Professional Features manual in Microsoft's Visual Basic Professional 3.0 documentation set.

The index provides a much better view of the information available in this manual. Why did someone need to prepare such an exhaustive index? Well, I've heard that every major book of facts needs an index. In fact, I usually look into the index for guidance before looking anywhere else.

Somehow, the index supplied in this fine set of documentation wasn't up to the level that some people might like. This is an impressive index, mind you! It is nearly 20 pages of dual-column index entries, squeezed in with a font of only 8.5 points. That's a lot of entries, and the file is prepared in Microsoft Word for Windows, so you end up with a very nice presentation.

Think of how much work it would be to do this all by hand! Sometimes it's amazing what work people will do without any hope or expectation of recompense. Do you have a favorite project you've completed that could be shared? Sounds like the beginnings of a great shareware package!

```
┌─────────────────────────────────┐
│ ─     Hack Facts      ▼  ▲      │
├─────────────────────────────────┤
│ Visual Basic Variable        ▲  │
│ Naming and                      │
│ Programming Guide               │
│ Lori Walker                     │
│ Microsoft Corporation           │
│ Freeware, 21K                   │
│ CODEGU.ZIP                      │
│                              ▼  │
├─────────────────────────────────┤
│ ◄ │                         │►  │
└─────────────────────────────────┘
```

The Visual Basic Variable Naming and Programming Guide is another file dedicated to Visual Basic programmers, but with information that can be used by other language masters. This document, prepared in Windows Write format, describes naming conventions for variables, based upon the type of variable involved. This is an offshoot of pure Hungarian notation and provides a good basis for programmers in any language.

7

Beyond variable names, the document also describes naming conventions for menus, provides guidelines for setting environment options, discusses the formatting of your code, and talks about creating strings for use in message boxes, input boxes and SQL queries.

Standards? For BASIC?

What's going on here? We've spent years making BASIC go away. Professional programmers moved to any other language (Pascal, C/C++, Modula-2, FORTRAN, even COBOL), just so they wouldn't have to use (or say they use) BASIC. Windows and Unix were developed with C, so you had to know C to be a professional, right? Now what happens? One of the most popular (wildly popular, even) and productive environments for developing Windows programs is Visual Basic! Not only that, people are writing standards for the development of BASIC code. Where did we go wrong?

Enough with stuff for Visual Basic programmers. I know, there are many of you out there, but I know that other languages are used for Windows programming, so let's move on to information for the rest of us.

Most of the items listed in this section have been part of larger articles or collections with many interests in mind. There are also hundreds of smaller files, like the specific articles in the collections, which deal with a single topic. There are several of these types of articles included on the CD-ROM, and a few are listed here to get you started. These are not the types of things that people release as shareware, because it's too much work; it's just information someone wanted to share.

FILENAME	TOPIC OF DISCUSSION
CREATE.TXT	Creating a database with the Integra VDB controls and Borland C++
DLLCLA.ZIP	Using C++ classes in dynamic link libraries

FILENAME	TOPIC OF DISCUSSION
EDITBT.ZIP	Implementing an Edit button in database front-end applications using Visual Basic 3.0
O2SDI.ZIP	How to write a Windows SDI program in Borland C++ using OWL
O2SPLS.ZIP	How to write a Windows program with a Splash screen, in Borland C++ with OWL
UNDOC.ZIP	Undocumented Borland C++ tips

Most of the files in this section only come out once, or once in a while. In the next section, we'll talk about some files that are produced on a regular basis, and I therefore refer to them as Online Magazines.

Online Magazines

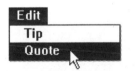

If computers take over (which seems to be their natural tendency), it will serve us right.
—*Alistair Cooke*

Some of the magazines you get may cause you trouble. I remember working for a manager who told me I got too much mail, and that I shouldn't worry about the industry; after all, my job was to develop software. Can you believe that this was at a well-known software company?

Well, I developed my own work-around. I started reading online magazines, like the ones mentioned in this section. These magazines are available electronically, either through download services or through CD-ROM collections. And the best part is that you read them by looking at the computer monitor, not by sitting back with your feet in the air!

The position is not as nice, and it's very difficult to read an electronic magazine during your morning constitutional, but if the boss sees you regularly studying the screen, you'll be known as someone who is really working hard! Just don't laugh too hard when you read the good stuff you find. And as for the sound effect samples some magazines include—be careful. A mooing cow in the middle of a software development office tends to draw curious stares, and then your cow will be out of the bag!

7

```
┌─────────────────────────────────────┐
│ ─        Hack Facts          ▼ ▲    │
├─────────────────────────────────────┤
│                                   ▲ │
│ Shareware Reference               █ │
│ Guide for Windows and             █ │
│ Windows NT                          │
│                                     │
│ Association of Shareware            │
│ Professionals                       │
│ 545 Grover Rd.                      │
│ Muskegon, MI  49442                 │
│ Freeware                            │
│ 682K                                │
│ SRGWN.ZIP                           │
│ 403K                                │
│ SRGNT.ZIP                         ▼ │
├─────────────────────────────────────┤
│ ← █                             → │
└─────────────────────────────────────┘
```

This first entry is not quite a magazine, but there is a lot here you'll want to see. The Shareware Reference Guide for Windows, and a similar guide for Windows NT, is produced on a regular basis by the Association of Shareware Professionals (ASP). The purpose of this huge help file is to showcase all the shareware that is available for Windows.

In this file, you can move through the different topics, looking at the files that are available, reading about features and capabilities, determining the associated costs for registration, and finding out what filenames to look for online, should you want to download a copy for your own testing (see Figure 7-2).

This is kinda like being a kid in a candy store. I went through the guide as part of my research for this book, and I can't wait to see my phone bill! There is so much good shareware being put out today that this guide should be one of the first places you look for new software.

There aren't a lot of catalogs for retail software that can compare with this collection. And being able to quickly search by name or topic is a great time-saver. Trying the

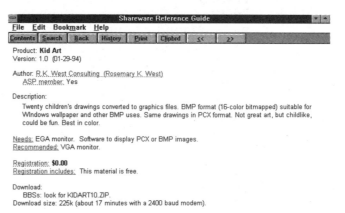

Figure 7-2.   *The Shareware Reference Guide offers complete information online for your shareware needs*

software before paying for it is great! How many bosses will tell you to buy software rather than try it first for free? Not many, I'll imagine. If yours does, let me know (there are a few programs I'd like someone to buy for me!).

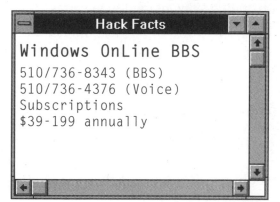

Hack Facts

```
Windows OnLine BBS
510/736-8343 (BBS)
510/736-4376 (Voice)
Subscriptions
$39-199 annually
```

The ASP updates the Shareware Reference Guide monthly. But there are also other sources of information about current shareware offerings. For instance, the WinOnLine Review and Windows Online "the Weekly" magazines don't only tell you programs exist, they give news and reviews about the software and the industry.

Windows OnLine is a bulletin board that caters only to Windows programs. You subscribe to the board and then have access to it in proportion to the donation you make. For instance, the SUPER membership allows for a maximum 2,000 files downloaded during the year, using up to 120 minutes and 5 MB per day. This is the ultimate membership for those who plan to get everything that's available.

If you're interested in downloading the magazines and trying out a few of the programs that are available (and discussed in the magazines), you can get by with one of their smaller memberships.

Be sure to read about VB Tips & Tricks in the previous section. It qualifies as a magazine, too.

The biggest problem you might have will be in reading all the information in these monthly magazines. As I mentioned, you cannot easily carry these magazines in your briefcase, and you can't spend every lunch hour reading program reviews (unless your project has been placed on hold).

One of the two magazines supplied and supported by Windows OnLine—WOLW (Windows Online "the Weekly")—is put out, believe it or not, weekly. There are several issues of this magazine on the CD-ROM. They have names like WOLW39.ZIP (Issue 39), WOLW40.ZIP, and WOLW43.ZIP.

Remember the names, because WOLW will be the base name for the weekly issues. These are weekly reports on the state of the Windows industry (see Figure 7-3). They cover both retail and shareware software, as well as the companies in the news.

the monthly edition, called WinOnLine Review, has additional reviews of software that is new or updated. It tells about shareware and retail software, and what is currently available for downloading from the WOL BBS.

There are a lot of good articles in these magazines. They are more than just lists of programs with bare detail (see Figure 7-4). They are enjoyable and full of information you can use. In addition, the reviews let you know how programs are regarded by the testers.

Naturally, the CD-ROM would be incomplete if there weren't copies of the monthly WinOnLine Review. So look for files with names like WOLR55.ZIP (Issue 55), WOLR69.ZIP, and WOLW75.ZIP.

And don't think that these are minor league players. These magazines are not at all small. The weekly is presented in

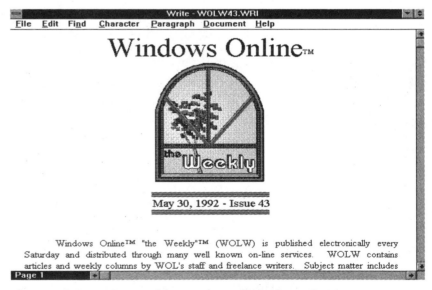

Figure 7-3.   *The weekly version of Windows OnLine news gives you lots to chew on during the week*

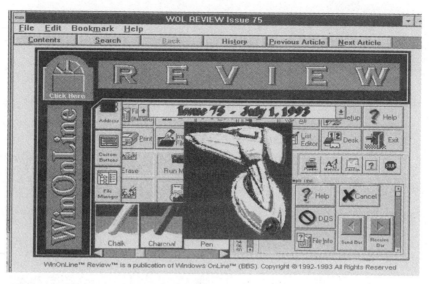

Figure 7-4. *Monthly news and reviews from Windows OnLine*

Windows Write (*.WRI) format, I guess so that you can print it out and carry it around during the week. The monthly editions are published as Windows Help (*.HLP) files. Issues are often into megabyte and multimegabyte sizes!

There have been other magazines. Modules & Definitions was about Modula-2 programming. Basically Visual was about Visual Basic programming. These no longer have new editions, but are often found in old CD-ROM collections. Do you know why these aren't published anymore? It's because people had such a good time reading them that they forgot to pay for them! The editors and writers of these magazines, as with other shareware authors, really need your support if they are to continue producing the best things for us to read and use. Think of shareware as a 30 Net billing. Try the program or magazine for 30 days, and then pay if you like it. If you don't like it, delete it from your system.

There is a lot of information available. How do you find out about more? Well, the first place to look is in some of the List files noted in the next section.

The flush toilet is the basis of Western civilization.
—Alan Coult

List of Lists

There are hundreds and hundreds of lists available on bulletin boards, electronic services, and CD-ROMs. Guess what? There is even a list for this book (see Appendix B), that tells all the files that are on the disk.

But also on this CD-ROM are lists of other software that is available. On most major electronic services (for example, CompuServe, bix, and America Online), in each of the special interest areas, someone will keep a file updated with a list of all the other files that are available in that area.

The names of these files of file lists are varied, and you can't always tell what they will be. On many CD-ROMs, the file might be ALLFILES.LIS, or FILES.BBS, common names used in many bulletin boards.

For specific areas on a major service, however, these will differ for each area. The following table shows some of the lists included on the CD-ROM with this book.

FILENAME	DESCRIPTION
BCW01.ZIP	List of files from Borland C++ for Windows area number one on CompuServe
BCW10.ZIP	List of files from Borland C++ for Windows area number ten on CompuServe
CPPU11.ZIP	List of C++ files available from the C++ Utility Library
FCAT04.TXT	List of files relating to CD-ROMs
FORUMS.ZIP	List of all the Microsoft Forums on CompuServe
MSLINDEX.ZIP	List of files available from the Microsoft Software Library (MSL)
VBINDEX.ZIP	List of files in the MSBASIC area on CompuServe
VBUTL.ZIP	List of Visual Basic files available as shareware or public domain
XWINFUN.ZIP	List of files in the Windows FUN area of CompuServe

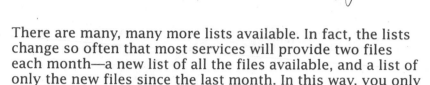

There are many, many more lists available. In fact, the lists change so often that most services will provide two files each month—a new list of all the files available, and a list of only the new files since the last month. In this way, you only need to get the updates each month.

Organizing and Beautifying

One last little topic for this chapter, before I let you go. There are lots of document files you might want to look at while you are running under Windows. You probably know that you can install them into Program Manager Windows, and let the correct file association display the file. What I mean is, if you add INFO.DOC to the Documents Group, Word for Windows will be called to display that file (if your associations are set up that way).

But what sort of icon do you see for your document file? Some of the magazines come with their own icons. But what if they don't? Never fear—there are thousands of icons available on the networks, and a whole bunch on the enclosed CD-ROM.

Here are just a few of the icon files included in this book:

FILENAME	DESCRIPTION
DEMOICON.ZIP	A collection of icons
ICOLIB02.ZIP	A collection of over 3,000 icons in 66 different categories
ICONS2.ZIP	Another icon collection
ICONS3.ZIP	Yet another icon collection
MOREICON.ZIP	And yet another collection, over 400 more icons

Yes, there are thousands of icons even on this disk. So, what do you do? One option is to use Paint Shop Pro (Chapter 2) to open each of these icon files separately, looking for the ones that appeal to you most.

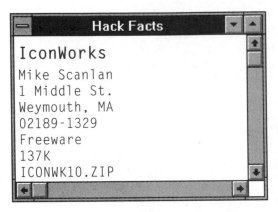

Icon Works is also useful for creating your own icons, and changing those that came with your applications (see Figure 7-5). It is a fully featured graphical editing package, with all the neat things you'd expect to see.

For instance, you can view the icons at any amount of zoom, moving in for really close work or moving out for a look at the overall design. It's easy with Icon Works to change colors of any pixels in your icon design. You can draw lines and circles. You can even fill areas with a paint bucket tool.

All in all, this is very similar in appearance and functionality to the wonderful painting program that comes free with each copy of Windows. The difference is that now you have a tool specially designed just for icons. Now, when you've completed you next great application, spend a little time defining the look of your program's icon.

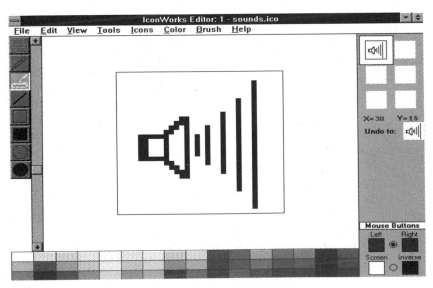

Figure 7-5. *You, too, can be an icon artist!*

Don't forget that icons have many other uses. You can assign them to your document files (as previously mentioned), and you can reassign the icons that came with your applications (after all, how long can you be expected to look at an icon that says "MS-DOS" and looks like it was created on a CGA graphics system?), so that your Program Manager begins to look personalized.

Hacking Ahead

Okay. This is the end of the line for you to be a passive reader. I hope you're using the CD-ROM by now, trying out this software as we go. But in the next chapter, things are going to change. It's time to start looking around on your own. In fact, I think it's time for a Pop-Quiz!

To think too long about doing a thing often becomes its undoing.

—*Eva Young*

7

8

Pop Quiz! Or, What Else Is New?

In the development of a superior programmer, curiosity about technical subjects must be a priority.
—Steve McConnell

You probably thought this book was going to be easy, that everything would be spelled out and well-organized, and all you'd have to do is reap the benefits. Well, I've tried to do this so far in the book, but now I want to give you a feel for what it is like to go online.

In this chapter, I'll tell you about some of my latest finds in the shareware world. I found most of these after I did the earlier chapters of this book, and I was just waiting to spring them on you now.

The items in this chapter are all jumbled together, not sorted by topic. Why? Because that's often how you find things on the electronic services, or on CD-ROM collections you might buy. However, since most BBSs are at least alphabetized in their file listings, I'll do the same here. I've left it up to you to look through and see what I've found. I think you'll enjoy the trip.

Hack Facts

How to Begin Programming in C/C++

Freeware
23K
C_START.TXT

Earlier, in Chapter 4, I spoke about learning C if you are going to be a Windows programmer. Remember, I did not say this was a requirement. But I do think that in order for you to get the maximum benefit out of the many examples, templates, articles, and demonstration programs available, you need to be able at least to read the C language.

179

Anyway, this is the topic of our first file, aptly titled "How to Begin Programming in C/C++." This is not a tutorial, but a guide to getting started in the actual learning process. It includes what books you might like to read, which compilers to look at, and what kinds of information you need to know to get started.

"It's a poor sort of memory that only works backwards," the Queen remarked.
—Lewis Carroll

I'm not sure who wrote this paper, but it is only eight pages long, so if you haven't made the jump into C or C++, this is a good place to start. The author covers what you need to get started, things to look out for, and what else you can expect to find to enhance your learning (tutorials, videos, online courses, classes to take at junior colleges and universities). The paper also describes the types of compilers available, the pros and cons of learning C before C++, and whether C should be taught as a first language.

I know, that seems like a lot of information to have in only eight pages. But it's a good overview, and worthy of a look if you are unsure of the path to take in acquiring C or C++ knowledge.

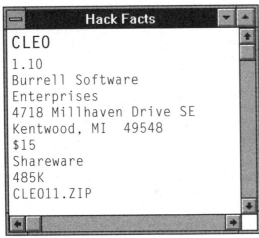

CLEO is a Convenient Little Environment Organizer, named for the programmer's dog (read about it in the files included). CLEO is a well-organized and well-thought-out approach to managing most of the things you'll have on your Windows desktop.

A menu bar at the top of the screen (see Figure 8-1) gives you access to many of the tools you need. For instance, in the Program Manager menu are all the files you have installed in the Program Manager, organized in the same groups that you have already defined.

Under the User menu, you can install your favorite programs, for quick access. There is also online help, and virtual screens! That's right, you now have eight screens with which you can work! Open Word for Windows in Screen 1, Visio in Screen 2, the Print Manager in Screen 3, and so on. Then, simply use the menus to select one of these complete screen layouts.

CLEO also places a status bar at the bottom of the screen. Why a status bar? Well, it shows the current status of your Windows resources (you can pick which resources to monitor), the disk space available on a selected drive, the current date and time, and the virtual screen you are in (in fact, click on the virtual screen number in the status bar, and you can quickly move to the other screens). CLEO also provides buttons for immediate access to the DOS command line, selection of a Windows command to execute, and exiting Windows.

Actually, this replaces several of the utilities and applications we've talked about thus far in the book. Or rather, it can replace them. It can also replace the Program Manager in many cases. But you may or may not like the pull-down menu approach, so just try it out for now, and then decide which tool or collection you prefer.

By the way, CLEO also comes with a program called CleoTask, a replacement for the Windows Task Manager. There are even instructions on how to install this as your default task manager (the program that pops up whenever you press the ALT+ESC combination and allows you to quickly move between the applications that are active).

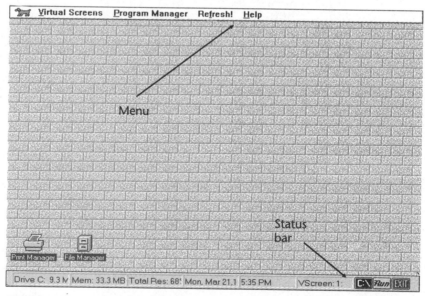

Figure 8-1. CLEO helps to organize your Windows world

```
Hack Facts

Code-A-Line

1.0
Optimax Corp.
P.O. Box 25447
Chicago, IL  60625-9998
$15-49
Shareware
452K
CODE.ZIP
```

Do you remember a neat little DOS program called ThinkTank? In my opinion, ThinkTank was one of the best programs ever for organizing your thoughts. It simply let you enter information in an outline form, and then organize it the way that you wanted.

ThinkTank was originally designed to help programmers. The theory was that you could use a top-down design by outlining all the functions your program had to perform, breaking them down into subfunctions, and so on, until you were at a level low enough that coding could begin.

ThinkTank had its clones (PC-Outline was a fantastic shareware competitor). Then, ThinkTank was merged with PC-Outline to create GrandView, and the saga seemed to end. But if you were looking for a Windows version, you had to wait. Now the wait may be over. Code-A-Line is a similar concept (see Figure 8-2) created for Windows use.

Code-A-Line was developed for programmers, but can actually be used by anyone who deals with structured information. Code-A-Line stores its files in an ASCII format, so moving from outline (structure) to implementation (coding) is a simple step.

there
is a simple method for using an outline processor like this for software design. Start by making your major functions outline entries at the topmost level (I, II, III, IV, and so on). Within each of these outline entries, start listing the subfunctions needed to perform the major processing. Then, continue to break these down into more and more detailed levels.

Eventually, you get to the point where the entries you have in your outline are ready to be turned into short subroutines. This is when you can start coding. What happens to the outline then? It becomes a road-map for development, and then a handy reference guide that can be placed into your documentation!

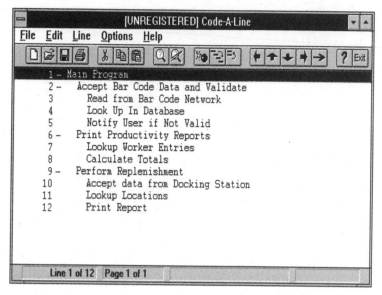

Figure 8-2. *Code-A-Line is an outline manager for program design, development, and more*

8

I know, I know. You don't have time to write documentation! That's why this outline becomes so important. And for maintenance, it can even serve as a table of contents to find where certain pieces of code may reside. Of course, for this to work, you need to update the outline when the coding is changed or completed. This continuous update involves real effort, but will certainly be worth it in the long run.

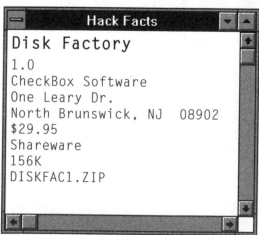

Disk Factory is another time and effort saver. Its premise is simple: if I'm using a multitasking environment, and my floppy drives are sitting idle, why not use them?

Disk Factory (see Figure 8-3) comes to the rescue, providing a disk-copying service and disk formatter that runs in the background while you continue your other tasks. Why use this instead of the wonderful File Manager that comes free with Windows? There are a couple of reasons.

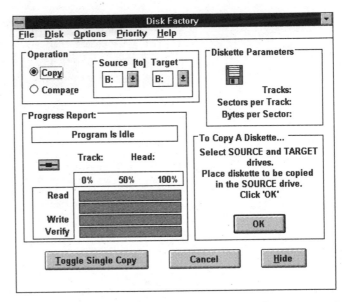

Figure 8-3. *Disk Factory provides copying and formatting in the background, so you can keep working (or playing)*

First, since Disk Factory is dedicated to only a few types of tasks, it can do them faster and more efficiently than File Manager; this means that you give up less of your processing capacity.

Second, Disk Factory makes the assumption that you don't need to be asked whether you really want to copy things (since you already asked to copy them once). Silly assumption, but one I don't mind. But there is an even bigger assumption you need to watch out for.

Everything is at the same time; nothing is vice versa.
—Zen saying

We all think in multiprocessing paths, right? That means that if we start a program (like File Manager) to do some task (like formatting or copying), we can go on to another task ourselves, and be able to run back and forth into File Manager to determine when the task has completed. Or maybe we're psychic and know immediately when things are done. In any case, Disk Factory assumes that we don't have that ability, and that we should be notified when it's time to change a disk, or when the copy has been completed. I'll tell you, this is an assumption I can definitely live with!

So if you need to copy or format disks, and would prefer to let your multitasking environment do it in the background (so you can be a bit more productive), *and* you would like to be notified when things are complete, try Disk Factory.

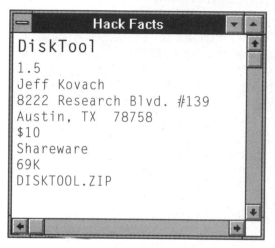

Hack Facts

DiskTool
1.5
Jeff Kovach
8222 Research Blvd. #139
Austin, TX 78758
$10
Shareware
69K
DISKTOOL.ZIP

There are sure a lot of tools out in sharewareland that do the things found in the Program Manager and File Manager, aren't there? Do you think this means something? I'm not sure, but I do know that these little tools, if installed so they can be accessed quickly, run faster and provide a great deal of additional functionality (or at least flexibility). One of the best little tools that falls into this category is DiskTool.

DiskTool provides a very small front-end with only a few options. You are able to Copy, Move, Erase, and Find files. That is most of the simple things I ever do, and bringing up the File Manager just to copy a new version of a file to the floppy disk seems like a bit of overkill, not to mention time-consuming.

since DiskTool is so small, you can probably leave it on your screen somewhere, and then it's always available. When you press the Copy or Move button, you can just select the source and destination and be done with it. The file moves without any further effort.

DiskTool also provides a one-button access to a Task Manager replacement. So, all you need is this little tool on your screen, and you will be able to handle a great portion of the file work you do in a day—and task switching! This is the type of tool I was talking about: simple, small, to the point, easy to learn, and inexpensive, too. Sometimes the time you save is well worth the small fee you pay for these great shareware tools.

8

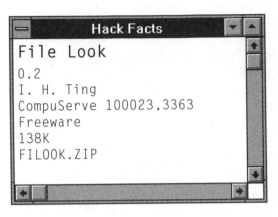

```
Hack Facts

File Look
0.2
I. H. Ting
CompuServe 100023,3363
Freeware
138K
FILOOK.ZIP
```

File Look is a wonderful package. No, it's not the best file-viewing package in the world. No, it doesn't have every feature you would ever want. No, it doesn't have fancy graphic screens to enlighten and enliven your workplace. So why is it so wonderful?

It's wonderful because of the attitude displayed by its programmer. Ting has spent some time learning about Visual C++, and in the process developed a file-viewing utility that he's called File Look.

Now here's the best part. He's sharing all his learning with you! This is not only a very capable, working program (as a file-viewing utility), but a great learning tool. A lot of the work has already been done for you, through the hands, eyes, and time of Ting.

did I mention that all the source code is included? See a feature that's missing? Add it, and then maybe you can release the changes, or send them to Ting for inclusion in any new releases.

In this day of everyone suing everyone, of "nothing for free," this is just an outstanding thing to do. Hopefully, more of this may happen in the future! Ting isn't the only one who has done this (remember the Pyramid game, in Chapter 4, which also came with source?). But it is refreshingly unusual enough that special attention should be paid.

Did you also notice that there isn't an address for sending shareware bucks? Just send Ting a message on CompuServe, thanking him for his attitude, even if you don't need the utility or use Visual C++. It's the thought that counts, and this is the type of attitude we need to advance the state of the art!

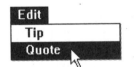

```
Edit
  Tip
  Quote
```

A lot of fellows nowadays have a B.A., M.D., or Ph.D. Unfortunately, they don't have a J.O.B.
— *Fats Domino*

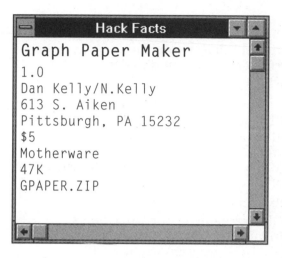

```
──        Hack Facts        ▼ ▲
Graph Paper Maker          ↑
1.0
Dan Kelly/N.Kelly
613 S. Aiken
Pittsburgh, PA 15232
$5
Motherware
47K
GPAPER.ZIP
                           ↓
◄ ▐                       ► ▐
```

Have you ever needed graph paper and searched in vain for it? Or found some graph paper that was ten lines to the inch, when you really wanted four lines per inch? Or wished you could have some paper that was 1/4-inch ruled vertically, but only ruled every inch horizontally?

Graph Paper Maker might be just the program you need. It doesn't do much, but if you need graph paper, it does a lot! You can specify the lines per inch in both horizontal and vertical directions (and yes, they can be different). You can also designate that after every so many lines, there should be a bold line. I've seen this used on commercial graph paper to mark off the inches, for instance. Just designate four lines per inch, with every fourth line being bold.

That's about it. You've just defined your graph paper. Now select Print, and the number of copies you want will start peeling off your printer. It only takes moments, and you've got exactly the right paper.

Tip

You may not want to print hundreds of pages of graph paper on your poor little printer. Create that custom look, and then take it to the Fast Copy Place down the street for lots of copies!

One other thing sets Graph Paper Maker out from the rest. (Well, ahead of the rest of shareware programs, anyway, because I'm not sure there are many graph paper design packages available.) This one is marketed as motherware. I know I didn't cover that one earlier, but that's because it isn't prevalent.

in motherware, the author (in this case, Dan Kelly) wants you to send any monies to his mother (N. Kelly). This may be a version of donorware (where the money is given to your favorite charity), but has a

8

special twist because Dan would like the money to go to his mother. Now, I don't know Dan or his mother, but I'm sure that there must be a special relationship for someone who would work hard to write a program, and ask that all the money go to his mother! Kudos, Dan.

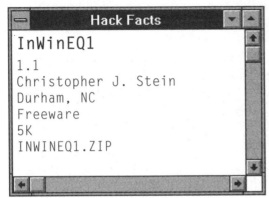

```
Hack Facts

InWinEQ1

1.1
Christopher J. Stein
Durham, NC
Freeware
5K
INWINEQ1.ZIP
```

Our next entry in the Pop Quiz is a piece of source code that originally appeared in the December 1991 *PC World* magazine. This code is now available on various bulletin boards and CD-ROMs and might be worth your attention.

Oh, the name of the program is InWinEQ1. Hold on to your horses, this is a DOS program, right here in a Windows book! It better be good, it better be wonderful, it better be something to do with Windows! Don't worry, it is.

This program is listed here because I wanted to show you that sometimes you will need to get out of the Windows mind-set to find all the programs and utilities you need as a Windows programmer.

InWinEQ1 is an assembly language program that determines whether Windows is already running. Why is this important? Not all programmers who do Windows programming do *only* Windows programming. And some programmers who do DOS programs still need to know what is going on with all these Windows computers that are available.

So InWinEQ1 was created. When run from the DOS command line, InWinEQ1 returns a 1 if Windows is running, and returns 0 otherwise. "How do it know?" the famous commercial writer once asked. Well, Windows creates an environment variable called "windir" when it starts. You'll notice that this variable name is in lowercase letters! This means that you cannot directly access it from the DOS command line, or within batch files, because DOS converts things.

```
Edit
 Tip
 Quote
```

He who wonders discovers that this in itself is wonder.
—M. C. Escher

Using an example from the InWinEQ1 documentation, this is a use of the program:

```
@ECHO OFF
InWinEQ1
IF ERRORLEVEL 1 GOTO INWINDOWS
CHKDSK! %1 %2 %3
GOTO DONE
:INWINDOWS
CLS
ECHO You cannot run CHKDSK from inside Windows!
:DONE
ECHO ON
```

This is a simple-to-use program, which comes with assembly language source code, a quick listing you can dump into DEBUG (without using an assembler), and other background on how and why it works.

Hack Facts

InfoPop/Windows

1.01
Clyde W. Grotophorst
GMUtant Software
Route 1, Box 296
Hamilton, VA 22068
Freeware
189K
IPWIN.ZIP

I talked about the Internet at several points throughout this book. It's the big network of networks that everyone is talking about these days. But how do you learn more about the Internet? Do you go out and buy a couple of books, or pay a consultant for some time? How about a free tutorial on the CD-ROM with this book?

If you chose the third option, you're in luck. InfoPop/Windows is a help-file-based tutorial about the Internet, complete with some valuable addresses. Simply select IPWIN.HLP from your File Manager (or Command Post, or whatever filer you are using), and the Windows Help system will display the file, in all its hypertext glory.

This is actually a good overview of the Internet system. Sections called "What is the Internet?," "BBS systems on the Internet," and "FTP" describe many of the overall topics you'll need to know. You'll find a discussion of how to get

8

If you aren't sure what all these terms mean, your best bet is to look at InfoPop/Windows!

your own Internet connection. There is also information about some of the Internet tools, like Archie and Gopher.

You can also learn about library catalogs, and library-oriented lists and serials. Other topics include Internet destinations, RFC documents, Telnet, WHOIS, Bitnet, and other well-known services that interconnect with the Internet.

The Glossary includes definitions for terms like Archie, Clarkson drivers, client/server, ethernet, file server, ftp, gateways, gopher, internet, ip address, listserver, nren, OPAC, packet switching, tcp/ip, telnet, Veronica, vt100, usenet, and wais.

If you've been wanting to learn about the Internet, here is a great place to start. After going through InfoPop/Windows, you'll have a much better idea where to go next in your search for Internet knowledge.

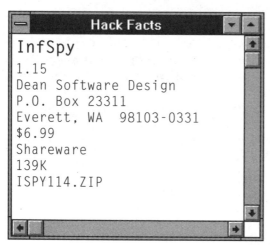

InfSpy
1.15
Dean Software Design
P.O. Box 23311
Everett, WA 98103-0331
$6.99
Shareware
139K
ISPY114.ZIP

A couple of utilities we've talked about before show some of the innards of Windows applications as they are running. One of the best utilities I've found that answers most of the questions is InfSpy (see Figure 8-4).

There is so much information available from InfSpy that I hesitate to try to list it all. Therefore, just realize that the list I'm reciting is not complete; it's just a taste of what you can expect.

In the top scroll area are all the global heap segments. If you double-click on any of these areas, you will be presented with the actual bytes in that area. So if you have a program gone awry, you can easily check the data that the program is using. For each of the global areas, you can also check for local heaps.

The next scroll area presents a list of the active windows. Selecting one of these windows (by double-clicking, of course) shows you the detail about that window. This includes the Windows and class style properties, the different handles being used, the parent and child rectangle coordinates, and more.

```
┌─────────────────────────────────────────────────────────────────────────┐
│ ─                    InfSpy - Windows Spy <unregistered>              ▼   │
├───────────────────────────────────────────────────────────────────────── │
│ Print   Unload Module   Terminate Task   LocalHeap   HeapInfo   Memory   Help │
│          Handle  Size  DPL C/D R/W Flags Address  Loc Type      Owner      │
│ Global  ┌0087   20480 03 data R/W U A L 80C5:4000                        ▲┐│
│ Heap:   │008F 1048576 03 data R/W U N I 0000:0000                         ││
│         │0097    4096 03 data R/W U A L 8062:6000                         ││
│         │009F     768 03 data R/W U A L 80CB:22A0      Unknown   GDI       ││
│         │00A7   33504 03 data R/W U A L 80F8:A840      Unknown   KERNEL   ▼┘│
│          Handle Type       Parent Task    Class+Name                      │
│ Active  ┌0F34  Top Level 0000   2A1F  <#32768> <>                        ▲┐│
│ Windows:│0EF4  Top Level 0000   0667  <#32771> <>                         ││
│         │4740  Top Level 0000   2327  <InfSpy> <InfSpy - Windows Spy <un  ││
│         │47A0  Child      4740   2327  <Button> <&Close>                   ││
│         │47E4  Child      4740   2327  <ListBox> <>                        ││
│         │4880  Child      4740   2327  <Static> <Name                     ▼┘│
│          Handle Parent Module      Name                                    │
│ Windows ┌1F67  0667   0817     CLIPSRV                                    ▲┐│
│ Tasks:  │27F7  0667   2837     WINCAP                                      ││
│         │1F3F  0667   1F5F     PRINTMAN                                    ││
│         │0667  013F   0677     PROGMAN                                     ││
│         │080F  0667   081F     NETDDE                                      ││
│         │2857  2A1F   2B47     CLEO                                       ▼┘│
│          Name             Handle Count   Loaded from Path                  │
│ Loaded  ┌ATM              07DF   1     "C:\WINDOWS\SYSTEM\ATM32.DLL"      ▲┐│
│ Modules:│ATMSYS           0147   2     "C:\WINDOWS\SYSTEM\ATMSYS.DRV"      ││
│         │BW_TM10          2EDF   1     "D:\WINAPPS\NAUTCD\NCDTIMES.FON"    ││
│         │CLEO             2B47   1     "D:\BOOK037\EXTRAS\CLEO11\CLEO.E    ││
│         │CLEOHOOK         2E3F   1     "D:\BOOK037\EXTRAS\CLEO11\CLEOHO    ││
│         │CLEOPM           2E4F   1     "D:\BOOK037\EXTRAS\CLEO11\CLEOPM   ▼┘│
│                        [  Close  ]    [  Refresh  ]                         │
└─────────────────────────────────────────────────────────────────────────┘
```

Figure 8-4.   *InfSpy lets you look into everything running under Windows, and even lets you play around with things you shouldn't*

This is useful for seeing how windows are set up from other people's applications, too!

The next area presents the Windows tasks that are running. Select one of these and you learn the task details, including parent information, the handles that are being used in relation to the tasks, stack information for the task, and much more.

The final area of the main window shows the modules that are loaded (for example, DLLs). You get all the detail about these modules if you select them. This includes the filename from which they were loaded, as well as the file date and time, and file size for the module.

Let's move to the main menu. There are options for unloading modules and terminating tasks, but if you use these, be careful; you may upset the balance that Windows manages so precariously, causing immediate system failure. I'm not trying to scare you or anything, just letting you know that caution is well-advised!

InfSpy also offers options for viewing the heap information and memory. You can look at the user or GDI heap areas, the percentage of free space on each, segment handles, space available on the heap, the number of items on the heap, and more. For memory, you get to see the amount of linear memory space, the amount free, the largest contiguous area that is free, the maximum available and maximum lockable pages, the number of pages that are unlocked or not in use, and the number of pages being managed. In addition, you get to see the swap file size (which seems to be a secret, unless you make a great effort to traverse the innards of 386 setup choices in the Control Panel).

If that isn't enough information, there is still more. But I'll let you find it on your own.

Make sure you're sitting down. Sit back and relax. Take a break and stir up those creative juices. I'm going to introduce you to a wonderful artist's package that is extremely fun for anyone, even a programmer on a break.

Matisse In Gray is a black, white, and gray-scale version (see Figure 8-5, which is only black and white and gray anyway, but which shows you a real version of what your screen might look like) of Matisse (a full-color version). Fauve Software has released the Gray version to show everyone what their software is like, in hopes that you will upgrade to the full-color Matisse package.

Why is Matisse different? We all have a drawing tool that comes with Windows, and many people have something more (Paint, Canvas, Corel, or one of the more unwieldy drawing packages). But Matisse is different. Matisse is more of an artist's tool. You don't just get to draw things, you get to pick the *realistic* tools to do so.

for instance, in some drawing packages, you can change the width of a line or the pattern used to draw it (striped, plaid, solid, and so on). But in Matisse, you can draw with chalk, crayon, or pencil. You can do some wonderful things with a calligraphy, felt-tip, or quill pen.

When you get ready to paint, use oils, water colors, chameleon (paint that changes colors), Japanese (like the

Figure 8-5. *Matisse will have you feeling like an artist in no time*

finely detailed drawings you see in the restaurants), surfaces, cubist, pastels, or even an airbrush. Wait, don't start painting yet—you can change the size, shape, and orientation of your brush. You can even change the density (color, in the color version, I expect) of the paint.

Matisse provides a Stamp function, for pressure stamping that you might do with a transfer medium, a felt-tip pen, or with an airbrush. There are even stroke and dot options you can use. You have the option to shape and manage any tool you use.

Okay, this is just a black and white (and gray) painting tool. But after a few times, you'll think your artistry is growing. The tools make a real difference, and Matisse is quite easy to learn and enjoy.

Beyond bringing simple pleasure, this package can come in handy for brochures, manuals, graphics, and much more. While you may think having no color is a handicap, most of us still don't have color printers, so it's not much of a problem. And if you want color, Matisse's price is very reasonable, compared to most of the other packages

A man paints with his brains and not with his hands.
—*Michelangelo*

available. Take a look at Matisse, and be sure to set aside some time to play!

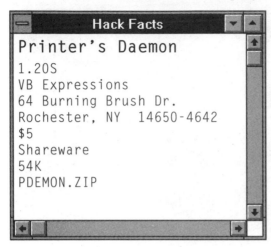

Now we move to a tool designed to ease your use of the File Manager for routine tasks, like maybe printing files! The Printer's Daemon is a drag-and-drop printing program. Short, simple, and sweet—that's all there is.

Why would you want this package? You may have noticed that there isn't much of a facility in the File Manager for printing your files. Sure, you can double-click on the file, and wait for the correct (appropriate, or at least assigned) application to come up, and then select the file (if it hasn't been done automatically), and then ask it to print, and verify that you want one copy, and that you want to use the default printer, and then shut all the programs down again. *And all you wanted was a listing of one page of code!*

I've used compilers that take 30 seconds to a minute to start up, and then they bring up all the files you were working on before, and so on. I know, I could turn some options off, but then when I really need to use the compiler, it's not set up correctly.

So back to the Printer's Daemon. Imagine a different scenario. You are looking through the File Manager, and aren't sure what a certain small C file is for. You can double-click on the filename, and bring up the entire compiler environment again. But that takes too long. So you simply click on the file, hold the button down, and drag the file icon to the Printer's Daemon icon.

the file starts printing. Boy, you say, that was easy. But what about selecting the printer you want to use? No problem, click on the Printer's Daemon icon, and you can choose to set up the printer.

You can also select an option to automatically bring up the File Manager when you start the Daemon. Then, if you know you need to print a file, just start the Daemon, and it will start the File Manager for you. Pick the file, drag, print, and you're done. Can life get any better?

Don't go overboard, though. Remember that a printing program can only print things it understands. Start sending EXE files, or even Ami Pro files to Printer's Daemon, and you'll end up with a lot of scrap paper!

```
┌──────────────────────────────────────────┐
│ ─     Hack Facts          ▼ ▲ │
├──────────────────────────────────────┬──┤
│ PC News                              │▲ │
│ Review—Windows Edition               │  │
│                                      │  │
│ Bolt Publishing                      │  │
│ 15600 NE 8th St.                     │  │
│ Suite B1-412                         │  │
│ Bellevue, WA  98008                  │  │
│ Freeware                             │  │
│ 39K                                  │  │
│ PNR_5.ZIP                            │  │
│                                      │▼ │
├──┬────────────────────────────────┬──┤
│ ◄│                                │► │
└──┴────────────────────────────────┴──┘
```

And now, back to the news. PC News, that is—Windows edition. This is a text file, a review of the news that is making history in our business arena. You can print it, read it, or store it. You can pass it to your friends. You can paper the bathroom walls with news of historical import.

Or you can just read it on a regular basis, and keep up with the market. The Windows edition is especially appropriate for those of us who work in Windows. It is published on a regular basis, so you can keep up with the changing world.

I know, you may think it's easier to just buy a local paper at the bus stop in the morning. But there are some problems with that. First, when you are in the midst of designing your next great application, do you really care who died? Or would you rather know what new standards were released for Windows messaging?

do you care that a certain auto body repair shop closed down for not paying back taxes, or would you rather know that a new version of your compiler has been released, because of all the problems with the previous release (yes, the one you are using for this latest, down-to-the-wire development project, the one with all the problems you can't seem to solve)?

Well, I'm sure the local news is good for you to know. After all, if the repair shop was currently working on your car, you might be in big trouble. And if the mechanic was the one who died (because your car fell on him), well, you get the picture.

8

Many of the quotes in this book were taken from programs like Sage. Many others came from books in my library. But if you use Sage, you can put all of them into the same front-end and read quotes whenever you want. The quotes come from advertisements, comic strips, TV shows and movies, and even famous people.

Sage looks different from other quote programs (see Figure 8-6). But that's good—it looks more like a three-dimensional Windows program (imagine that!).

Sage has several added touches that make it possibly the quotation program of choice for Windows. For instance, you have the ability to add any quotes to the data file that you might like. The whole file is in ASCII format, so you can quickly look at, edit, or add to the file. Suddenly, all of your own wit and wisdom can be showing up on a regular basis.

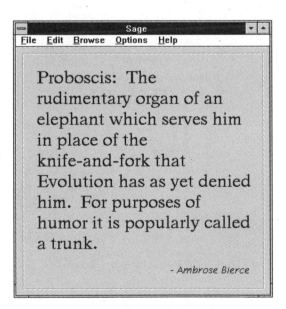

Figure 8-6. *Sage can be your constant companion and source of timeless wisdom*

Sage is inexpensive, especially for all of the quotes that come with the program. I was quite impressed by the nearly 5,000 quotes in the file, and you can add your own. By the way, adding your own is a simple process of typing it in, each quote on its own line. You can add a reference (who said it), and can even embed carriage returns for that finished look.

What makes Sage even more exciting is its ability to be used with OLE (object linking and embedding). That's right! Think about it—you can now embed timeless wisdom in your spreadsheets, so you'll always have something new to think about. Or better yet, give your coworkers something to think about each time they bring up their Excel applications. Remember, you could create your own quote data file, removing the existing 5,000-odd quotations and replacing them with corporate slogans, advertisements for local eateries, or simple nonsense. How about definitions of words (Internet words, for instance)? Every day, your fellow employees will become smarter and smarter, and no one will ever guess why.

Sage has a lot of possible uses beyond simple display of quotations. Think about it a while, and try it out. You'll have a lot of fun.

Hack Facts

```
SmartDoc
1.12
Oakley Data Services
3, Oakley Close
Sandbach
Cheshire CW11 9RQ
ENGLAND
£15
Shareware
99K
SMTDOC.ZIP
```

One pet peeve I have about Windows is that help files, while very useful in an interactive or context-sensitive way, are a real hassle to read cover-to-cover (so to speak). I'm sure that part of this is due to the fact that with a good printed copy of Windows help, some crafty people would try to get by with *illegal* copies of software, no longer needing a preprinted manual.

Well, I use *legal* copies of software, and sometimes I'd like to print the help files. For instance, from time to time I've been on a beta test where the help file *was* the documentation. It's really hard to study help files without your PC. Other times, I've gotten great shareware programs that are just help files with terrific hypertext connections, like InfoPop/Windows and several of the regular shareware magazines. I like to carry some of that stuff around with me, without carrying a PC. What to do?

in steps another specialized tool, SmartDoc. SmartDoc is designed to print help files. Imagine that! Printing stuff that you look at on the screen. This changes WYSIWYWLTG (what you see is what you would like to get) to WYSIWYG (what you see *is* what you get).

Using a unique method of printing help files, SmartDoc preserves the look of the screens. What it does is step through the help file one topic at a time, and "press" the "Print Topic" menu selection for each topic. Sure, you could do this on your own, but why not let the computer do some of the work for you (another unique concept!).

Remember, though, that if a help file uses multiple fonts, graphics, or other memory-consuming items, it might take a while to print the whole thing. In fact, the documentation for SmartDoc suggests that you start the project at the end of the day, and let it process and print overnight.

Simple problem, simple solution. The way software ought to be.

Here's another program that is to the point. But it is a whole lot more. Throughout this book, I've shown you some programs that perform the functions of the Program Manager, the File Manager, and even the Task Manager. Some are better, some have different functions, some are smaller and require less overhead.

But Tasker is something different. When installed and running, Tasker places a collection of buttons in the upper-right corner of your screen, kinda like the Next machine did. Whenever you start a new program, Tasker adds a new button. You don't have to do anything manually, it all happens without any work on your part.

Of course, when you close the application, Tasker takes the button back off the button bar. The buttons have the icon that is associated with each application, so it is easy to move from one task to another. The normal icon for a minimized application still shows at the bottom of the screen, as you might expect, but Tasker makes it easy to search for and switch to the tasks you have running.

With Tasker and DiskTool (discussed earlier), you can take up minimal screen space and gain great productivity. With the advent of the Super VGA (and beyond) resolutions, there is even more space available, so a few small tools permanently mounted in a corner of your screen become a welcome addition. For simple tasks there's no need to go through all the steps normally needed to bring up the File Manager or Program Manager.

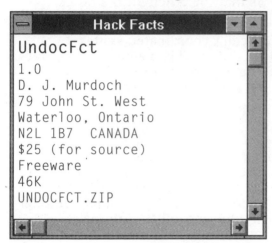

Hack Facts

UndocFct
1.0
D. J. Murdoch
79 John St. West
Waterloo, Ontario
N2L 1B7 CANADA
$25 (for source)
Freeware
46K
UNDOCFCT.ZIP

UndocFct is a special tool you may wonder about. Its purpose is to find the use of any undocumented Windows calls made in your (or other people's) programs.

Simply run your executable program through this program, and UndocFct will list all of the undocumented functions that are being used. There is also an option to print all of the functions, whether they are documented or not.

This may seem like a tool with little use, especially if you only plan to work from the Windows SDK (or equivalent software development kit from your favorite compiler vendor). But you might be surprised.

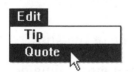

If the human mind were simple enough to understand, we'd be too simple to understand it.

—Pat Bahn

When you finish your next great application, use UndocFct to list all the Windows functions that you used. Now you have a valid piece of documentation for your programmer's notebook. What happens when you move to another version of the environment (for example, WindowsNT, Windows for Workgroups, Win-32, or a RISC derivative)? Simple, take the list with you and make sure that all of the functions are supported.

What about when the API changes? It never will, right? Just in case, now you can list all the functions you are using. The functions that were undocumented may become part of the API, while other API functions may be removed from the API, or become undocumented. You never know what might happen, but now you have a good handle on the functions you need to support.

(This is also a great way to keep track of your undocumented Windows functions.)

```
Hack Facts
WinEdit
3.0D
Wilson WindowWare, Inc.
2701 California Ave. SW #212
Seattle, WA  98116
$89.95-129.95
Shareware
1.6MB (installed with docs)
WE-30D.ZIP, WILREL11.ZIP,
DISCLAIM.ZIP
```

I know I told you about some editors for programmers in the early chapters of the book, but here is another one you might want to try. WinEdit was designed with the needs of programmers in mind and offers some tools that the other editors don't.

For instance, in a C program, you can have color-coordinated syntax highlighting. This means that variables can be one color, keywords a different color, and comments yet another color.

I used to think that this color syntax highlighting was just frivolous, until I found a variable name spelled incorrectly. By having the syntax color-coded I easily found the errors and quickly corrected them. This feature is even handier for keywords—if you spell them wrong, they won't show up in the keyword color! Several of the major compiler vendors are now supplying this capability with their environments, so there must be some value in using it.

Anyway, WinEdit also does the things you'd expect from a programmer's editor, like letting you compile and link your programs without leaving them. The retail version, which you get when you register, is also sold.

By the way, I talked earlier about reading some of the stuff that comes with shareware. Here is the disclaimer that comes with WinEdit: "Any similarity to real persons, living or dead, is purely coincidental. Void where prohibited. Some assembly required. List each check separately by bank number. Batteries not included. Contents may settle during shipment. Use only as directed. No other warranty expressed or implied. Do not use while operating a motor vehicle or heavy equipment. Postage will be paid by addressee. Subject to CAB approval. This is not an offer to sell securities. Apply only to affected area. May be too intense for some viewers. See store manager for further details. Do not stamp. Use other side for additional listings. For recreational use only. Do not disturb. All models over 18 years of age. If condition persists, consult your physician. No user-serviceable parts inside. Freshest if eaten before date on carton. Subject to change without notice. Times approximate. Simulated picture. No postage necessary if mailed in the United States. Breaking seal constitutes your acceptance of agreement. For off-road use only. As seen on TV. One size fits all. Many suitcases look alike. Contains a substantial amount of non-tobacco ingredients. Colors may, in time, fade. We have sent the forms which seem to be right for you. Slippery when wet. For official use only. Not affiliated with the American Red Cross. Drop in any mailbox. Edited for television. Keep cool; process promptly. Post office will not deliver without postage. List was current at time of printing. Return to sender, no forwarding order on file, unable to forward. Not responsible for direct, indirect, incidental or consequential damages resulting from any defect, error, or failure to perform. At participating locations only. Not the Beatles. Penalty for private use. See label for sequence. Substantial penalty for early withdrawal. Do not write below this line. Falling rock. Penalty for private use, $300. Lost ticket pays maximum rate. Your canceled check is your receipt. Add toner. Place stamp here. Avoid contact with skin. Sanitized for your protection. Be sure each item is properly endorsed. Sign here without admitting guilt. Slightly higher west of the Mississippi. Employees and their families are not eligible. Beware of dog. Contestants have been briefed on some questions before the show. Limited time offer, call now to insure prompt delivery. You must be present to win. No passes accepted for this engagement. No purchase necessary. Processed at location stamped in code at top of carton. Shading within a garment may occur. Keep away from fire or flame. Replace with same type. Approved for veterans. Booths for two or more. Check here if tax deductible. Some equipment shown is optional. Price does not include taxes. No Canadian coins. Not recommended for children. Prerecorded for this time zone. Reproduction strictly prohibited. No solicitors. No alcohol, dogs, or horses. No anchovies unless otherwise specified. Restaurant package, not for resale. List at least two alternate dates. First pull up, then pull down. Call toll free before digging. Driver does not carry cash. Some of the trademarks mentioned in

8

Edit
Tip
Quote

If builders built buildings the way programmers wrote programs, then the first woodpecker that came along would destroy civilization.

—Gerald Weinberg

this product appear for identification purposes only. Record additional transactions on back of previous stub. Do not fold, spindle or mutilate. Substantial penalty for early withdrawal. 25 city, 35 highway. Your mileage may vary." That should about cover it!

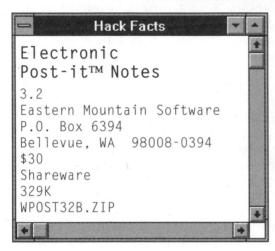

```
Hack Facts

Electronic
Post-it™ Notes
3.2
Eastern Mountain Software
P.O. Box 6394
Bellevue, WA  98008-0394
$30
Shareware
329K
WPOST32B.ZIP
```

What does your disk look like? How about your books and magazines? Are they filled with countless yellow notes, slightly sticky on one end? If so, don't fear—I think it's a national epidemic.

I get really upset with myself, however, when I make all these notes and have nowhere to put them so they won't get lost. Worse, I can only find the tablet half the time that I need it. Here is a solution that you might enjoy: Electronic Post-it™Notes.

These are pretty nifty. Once the program is run, it iconizes itself. Whenever you need a note, just double-click the icon. Up pops a note that you can place anywhere on your screen. They come up with a yellow background (for obvious reasons), but you can change it if you desire. After all, the paper version is available in other colors!

as with the paper versions, you can select the size you want. There are three default sizes, but the notes are in sizable windows, so you can actually make them any size. You can define whether the notes always stay on top (unlike your paper version), or get covered like any other Windows window.

In addition, you can save and restore these notes to a disk file. You can even have them be saved automatically every few minutes, in case you forget. This is what my desk needs, automated Post-it™notes!

So break out this program, start collecting all those notes on your desk, type them in, save them to disk, and you won't lose any more important info! Don't forget to color-code them, so you know which ones were most important. Sounds like magic, doesn't it?

Hack Facts

PrintDir

David Foster
184 Eckford St. #3
Brooklyn, NY 11222
$10
Shareware
23K
WPRNDIR.ZIP

Here's another piece of magic you might be interested in. PrintDir is an add-on for the File Manager that allows you to print out directory listings. Sure, that doesn't seem like much, but why can't you do it any other way? You can always drop to DOS, right?

PrintDir is a DLL file that you put in your Windows System directory. Then, go into your FILEMAN.INI file, make a few changes, and PrintDir is a permanent addition to your File Manager menu (see Figure 8-7).

There are several options available for PrintDir. For instance, you can print all the files in a directory, sorted by name. Or print all the files sorted by the file's size or date. These are standard types of requests, wouldn't you think? Well, you can also print just the files you have selected. This is handy when the boss (yours, or the client—either way, the boss) wants to see how much code you've pumped out over the

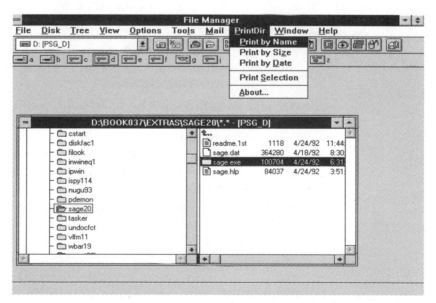

Figure 8-7. *PrintDir nestles quietly in your File Manager menu, just waiting to print directory listings for you*

last few hours, and wants a listing of the C, C++, and header files *only*. After all, there's no time to figure out which files are source (that's the excuse, anyway).

PrintDir installs in minutes, provides a very useful addition to the File Manager, and doesn't cost much. It would be nice if more of these programs were around. I'd like to see a File Manager add-on that allows you to browse or print a file. There are drag-'n'-drop programs that do this (see Printer's Daemon earlier in this chapter), but a consolidated approach, with all the tools in one place—and without the need to hunt for the icons of all the add-ons—would certainly be nice.

WinTune is a program that was developed by *Windows Magazine*. It is basically a big testing and benchmark program. With WinTune, you can see how your system is running and maybe even find ways to improve your performance.

Windows Magazine has done a good job of providing free software to its readers (and others who are interested enough to find it). This is another of the fine tools in this line of excellence.

WinTune offers a set of comprehensive tests, a simple check-up, or individual tests that check specific items in your Windows environment.

WinTune is subtitled "The Windows Magazine Test & Tune-up Kit," and its help along those lines includes testing for your CPU, floating-point processor, memory, and disk drives. You can select any or all of these tests. In all cases, your results will be compared against an appropriate standard.

The program itself is not very large. The biggest use of disk space is in the tuning tips that are found in the help file. Any time you run a test, you can ask for tips on how to improve, or tune, your results.

One of the nicest things I found was the phone numbers of many of the more popular video board manufacturers. Since much of the video speed is related to the driver in use, the tips suggest calling your video board manufacturer's bulletin board system to find out if there is a newer driver available.

I even found one for my board, and although it was a beta copy, it seems to help. I never would have known about this if I hadn't asked for tips on speeding up my video performance.

Since *Windows Magazine* doesn't charge for this software, I suppose you could go out and buy a magazine or two, or even subscribe. I'm sure they would be thrilled, and maybe they'd keep developing this free stuff for us all.

Hack Facts

Interactive Yellow
Pages & Network
Auction
Lighthouse Productions
P.O. Box 7885
Santa Cruz, CA 95061
Freeware
163K
YELLOW.ZIP

Of course, there are a lot of companies that you may wish to reach, who will not show up in the WinTune help and tips. For instance, most software vendors have little to do with how your hardware runs. So, turn to the Yellow Pages.

No, not the Yellow Pages in your phone book. I'm talking about the Interactive Yellow Pages & Network Auction, a help file that is available on this CD-ROM. It's not everyone you'll ever need to contact, but it is updated regularly, so once you get into the habit of looking for shareware, you'll be able to keep up to date.

Not only that, you can get your own listing in the Interactive Yellow Pages. A simple listing is free, but since the whole system is based on a Windows help file, you can also buy "quarter page" and "full page" advertising. Naturally, this refers to a screenful of data for each full-page ad. Once you are listed, you may find yourself in front of 50 million viewers! That is the number of viewers quoted in the documentation for the Interactive Yellow Pages; after all, the Network Auction is based on all of the advertising you and others purchase.

It's a handy reference. All companies are listed in topical areas, as you might expect from Yellow Pages. For instance, look in the Vertical Markets area for those specialty programs you need. There are also areas for hardware and software.

This is one of those files I might like to print with SmartDoc (discussed earlier in this chapter), so I could carry the phone

8

numbers in my briefcase. Of course, I don't have a briefcase, but if I did, I'd like to have this with me when I go on site for installations. Then, if I were having problems, I could call anyone I deemed necessary.

Hacking Ahead

I guess you're on your own now. This book was designed to get you a pile of software to try, and let you know what types of things are available. In Chapter 1, you learned about how to find even more software. And in this chapter, you started out on a discovery journey of your own.

If you haven't started looking at the stuff on the CD-ROM, give it a shot. Appendix A tells you all about installing and using the CD, so you should have no trouble. Then, hook up with a modem (or a friend with a modem), and keep looking for the newest tools available.

But don't forget! Much of this software is *shareware*, and the authors who have spent time producing this software—the tools, the games, the sound clips, and all the rest—are expecting to be paid for their work. If you use a tool and it makes you work better (or play better), be sure to pay the registration fees! This helps the shareware industry to grow. In addition, it provides competition (both in features and in price) for retail software, giving us, in the end, the best of all worlds.

ROM on!

"Oh dear, I think you'll find reality's on the blink again."
—Marvin, the Paranoid Android

Installation of the CD-ROM

Did you read this book yet? Or are you skipping to the end to see how it turns out? If you fall into the latter category, move on to the next appendix, and you'll see everything that is on the CD-ROM. After all, the CD-ROM bound into this book contains all the files described in the various chapters.

Finding What You Want

There are three ways to find something that might interest you. First, you can read the book and write down the names of the files that sound interesting to you.

Second, you can browse through Appendix B and look for the descriptions that sound interesting. From here, look at the chapter in which a program was discussed, and you'll find out more about it before actually pulling it from the disc.

Third, for those of you who hate to read, and who turned here so they wouldn't have to read at all, just put the CD-ROM in your CD-ROM drive, and then run the WINCOOK1 application on the CD-ROM (see Figure A-1). This program contains an online version of Appendix B, and also is fun to navigate through. It includes a lot of information online about some of the materials available for learning more about Windows programming (and other stuff, too).

Figure A-1. *The WINCOOK1 will walk you through the contents of the CD-ROM*

Getting Something Out of Nothing (Zip, That Is)

Most of the files are compressed on the disc. Therefore, you will need to decompress them (also known as unarchiving, de-archiving, or unZipping) before they will be of any use. There are several steps to this process.

First, look for the file you want. If you read about a program in the book that sounds interesting, look at the Hack Facts box, and jot down the name of the archive file you need. Alternatively, if you remember a name, and weren't sure what chapter it was in, look in Appendix B, which lists all the files alphabetically.

Usually, the file you want will end with the three-letter extension ZIP. This means that all the files you need have been compressed into a single file—the Zip file.

To extract the files from the Zip, use the WinZip program. This excellent program is described in Chapter 2 and has been placed in the top-level directory of the CD-ROM for quick access. Simply start the program, press the Open button, and navigate through the directories until you find the file you need.

When you find the file you want, press the Extract button. You will again navigate through the directories, this time searching for a location in which to place all the files extracted from your selected Zip file. By the way, if you specify a subdirectory that doesn't yet exist, WinZip will automatically create it before decompressing your Zip file.

Special Files You Might Need

A little learning is a dangerous thing.
—Alexander Pope

Many of the programs on the CD-ROM also require the use of certain files, notably VBRUN100.DLL, VBRUN200.DLL, and VBRUN300.DLL. These are special files used by applications that have been written in Visual Basic. Because of their common use, these three files have also been placed in the top-level directory of your CD-ROM, rather than being included in every program Zip file. To use these files, simply copy them to your WINDOWS\SYSTEM directory.

If you've worked with shareware before, you may already find that one or more of these files exist on your drive; don't worry, just keep the file with the latest (most current) date. You only need one copy of each of these files (one of the advantages of the Windows programming environment), so you may just want to copy all three files now. Then you won't have to worry about them later.

By the Way (or, As the World Turns...)

Appendix B lists all the programs that are on the CD-ROM that came with this book. However, because of production schedules, online delays, and a myriad of other time-consumers, there may be a few file names that look different. For instance, you may find an EXE file instead of a ZIP file. Don't panic! The EXE is a self-extracting file, meaning that if you run it from within Windows (or in DOS), the files will extract themselves.

A

You might also find a few version numbers have changed. In an effort to make this book and CD-ROM as up to date as possible, I often got shareware revisions long after the chapters were completed. So, you may find PROG220 rather than PROG200; stay calm and relaxed! There aren't many of these that didn't get changed, and the archives always start with the same few letters. Just think of this as an added bonus: the newest versions of software, at no extra cost!

Shareware at Its Best

Don't forget that most of these programs are *shareware*, which means that you need to pay for them if you end up using them regularly. Rates are reasonable, and you already have fully functional demonstrations from which to make decisions. Help support the shareware concept, so that more of this excellent software can be created and distributed.

Now, install the disc, read the book, and have some fun. After all, isn't that what programming is supposed to be about?

I think there's a world market for about five computers.
—Thomas J. Watson, Chairman of the Board, IBM (circa 1948)

Alphabetized List of Programs on the CD-ROM

Chapter	Filename	Description
5	3DXWD.ZIP	3-D crossword puzzle game with nice graphics
5	A.ZIP	WAV files starting with A
2	ABV30.ZIP	*Above & Beyond*, an information manager
2	ACCTMN13.ZIP	*Account Manager*, time tracking manager
2	ACHART12.ZIP	Programmer's ASCII/ANSI chart for Windows
2	ADRES1.ZIP	Address book
2	ALVIDA.ZIP	Quick exit from Windows
5	AMAZE321.ZIP	3-D maze game for Windows
6	APLANR.ZIP	A project and event planner
3	ATBSB001.ZIP	Toolbar and status bar DLLs
5	B.ZIP	WAV files starting with B
5	BARTEYE2.ZIP	Bart Simpson eyes that follow your mouse cursor

Chapter	Filename	Description
5	BCUBES.ZIP	*BrainCubes,* game that tests your memory
7	BCW01.ZIP	List of files from Borland C++ for Windows area 1 (CompuServe)
7	BCW10.ZIP	List of files from Borland C++ for Windows area 10 (CompuServe)
5	BDD.ZIP	*Battles in a Distant Desert,* game
5	BIOGRF.ZIP	*BioGraf,* biorhythm viewing and interpretations
4	BITMAP.ZIP	Bitmap and icon viewer with source
5	BRAINJ.EXE	*Brain Jam,* solitaire card game
5	C.ZIP	WAV files starting with C
2	CDPLY.EXE	Simple CD player for Windows
2	CDW210.ZIP	CD player for Windows
4	CHKDAT.ZIP	Validates dates, source
8	CLEO11.ZIP	Convenient Little Environment Organizer
2	CLOCKR23.ZIP	*Clocker,* run programs at requested times
8	CODE.ZIP	*Code-A-Line,* outlining program
7	CODEGU.ZIP	Visual Basic Variable Naming and Programming Guide
3	CODEPR.ZIP	*CodePrint,* file printing utility for programmers
5	CONCEN.ZIP	*Concentration Solitaire,* card game
5	COWS.ZIP	Cows screen blanker, with sound and random chickens
2	CP_8011.ZIP	*Command Post,* File Manager replacement
7	CPPU11.ZIP	List of C++ files available from the C++ Utility Library
7	CREATE.TXT	Creating a database with the Integra VDB controls and Borland C++
8	C_START.TXT	How to begin programming in C/C++

Chapter	Filename	Description
5	D.ZIP	WAV files starting with D
4	DATEMA.ZIP	Date math routines, includes work-day calculations
7	DATIDX.EXE	Index for Visual Basic Data Access Guide
3	DBPUTS.ZIP	Manage messages from programs using client-server approach
4	DDEMGR.ZIP	DDE Manager class, with source for C++
7	DEMOICON.ZIP	A collection of icons
5	DIALWORD.ZIP	Check the words you can make from a phone number
4	DIBPRT.ZIP	Returns a DIB and prints current window, in C
8	DISCLAIM.ZIP	WinEdit disclaimers
8	DISKFAC1.ZIP	Program to copy and format disks in background
8	DISKTOOL.ZIP	Program to copy, move, and find files
7	DLLCLA.ZIP	Using C++ classes in dynamic link libraries
6	DOUPRO20.ZIP	*Doughboy Install*, installation program
5	DS101.ZIP	*DinoSlot*, slot machine action with dinosaurs
5	DS9.ZIP	Computer responses from "Star Trek:Deep Space Nine"
4	DVLD11.EXE	Date validation routines, source
5	E.ZIP	WAV files starting with E
7	EDITBT.ZIP	Implementing an Edit button in database front-end applications using Visual Basic 3.0
5	ENTD1.ZIP	Bitmap image of *Enterprise*
2	EWARC.ZIP	*E! for Windows*, editor
2	EWCT3D.ZIP	*E! for Windows*, 3-D controls add-on
2	EZ-SET.ZIP	*EZ-Setup*, run SETUP or INSTALL from floppies automatically

B

Chapter	Filename	Description
5	F.ZIP	WAV files starting with F
7	FCAT04.TXT	List of files relating to CD-ROMs
6	FFBMGR.ZIP	*Financial Freedom Billing Manager*, for any kind of bill tracking
8	FILOOK.ZIP	File viewing program with Visual C++ source
5	FINSAV.ZIP	*FinTec*, screen saver program
3	FLAT.ZIP	Flat-file data manager with full source
7	FORUMS.ZIP	List of all the Microsoft Forums on CompuServe
2	FPRNT.ZIP	*Font Print*, print font examples
5	FRACT6.ZIP	Bitmaps generated with FractInt (fractals)
5	FRACT7.ZIP	More fractal bitmaps
5	FRACT8.ZIP	Even more fractal bitmaps
5	FRACT9.ZIP	Still more fractal bitmaps
4	FRES20.ZIP	*FreeRes*, shows status of Windows environment
2	FSP530.ZIP	*FontSpec Pro*, font management programs
5	G.ZIP	WAV files starting with G
5	GARFBMP.ZIP	Bitmap image of Garfield the cat
4	GETCPU.ZIP	Assembler source to determine CPU type
3	GETYOU.ZIP	*GetYour$*, Visual Basic DLL for gathering program registration information
4	GJV3D.ZIP	3-D wire frame routines
5	GLOBEBMP.ZIP	Full color bitmap of the globe
8	GPAPER.ZIP	Program to generate custom graph paper
3	GREP14.ZIP	Windows version of GREP string search utility
5	H.ZIP	WAV files starting with H

Chapter	Filename	Description
6	HELPED.ZIP	*Help Edit*, an editor for creating Help files
6	HOG101.ZIP	Limits machine resources for testing
2	HPLABL.ZIP	Label diskettes with HP laser and ink-jet printers
5	I.ZIP	WAV files starting with I
7	ICOLIB02.ZIP	A collection of over 3,000 icons in 66 different categories
7	ICONS2.ZIP	Another icon collection
7	ICONS3.ZIP	Yet another icon collection
7	ICONWK10.ZIP	*Icon Works*, icon designer and viewer
2	IMPST101.ZIP	*Imposter*, DOS command line replacement
2	INFVU144.ZIP	*InfView*, large file viewer with hex mode
6	INSTAL.ZIP	*Champion Install*, installation program
8	INWINEQ1.ZIP	DOS program to see if Windows is running
8	IPWIN.ZIP	*InfoPop/Windows*, an Internet tutorial
8	ISPY114.ZIP	View all kinds of information about Windows tasks, etc.
5	J.ZIP	WAV files starting with J
5	JUPITER2.ZIP	Collage of Jupiter and the Moon from *Voyager*
5	K.ZIP	WAV files starting with K
5	KAL16.ZIP	*Kaleidoscope*, excellent (!) screen saver
2	KILL15.ZIP	Task killer
5	L.ZIP	WAV files starting with L
3	LGFIL1.ZIP	Log messages to a file
4	LINETO.ZIP	*LineToy*, 3-D wire drawing tool
3	LIST10.ZIP	Pascal
5	M.ZIP	WAV files starting with M
2	MAGCAT14.ZIP	Magazine catalog program to track articles, books, etc.

B

Chapter	Filename	Description
5	MAGIC.ZIP	Domino game with mathematical overtones
4	MARQUE.ZIP	Add a marquee to your Windows
8	MATISSE.ZIP	Excellent gray-scale artists package
2	MEGAED.ZIP	*Mega Edit*, programming editor
5	MERC1BMP.ZIP	Bitmap image of Mercedes 560 SEL sedan (on your wish list?)
3	MF-DB.ZIP	Multiuser database manager for Windows languages
5	MMTREK.ZIP	Star Trek multimedia screen blanker
7	MOREICON.ZIP	And yet another collection, over 400 more icons
7	MSLINDEX.ZIP	List of files available from the Microsoft Software Library (MSL)
5	MYCATS.ZIP	*Cat!* and *TopCat!* follow your mouse cursor
5	N.ZIP	WAV files starting with N
5	NATLBMP.ZIP	Assorted bitmaps of subjects from nature
5	NCC1701A.ZIP	Bitmap image of original *Enterprise*
5	NCC1701D.ZIP	Bitmap of *Next Generation Enterprise*
5	NEKO20.ZIP	Cat that follows your mouse cursor
4	NEWTRA.ZIP	Memory allocation tracking for C++ programmers
5	O.ZIP	WAV files starting with O
7	O2SDI.ZIP	How to write a Windows SDI program in Borland C++ using OWL
7	O2SPLS.ZIP	How to write a Windows program with a Splash screen in Borland C++ with OWL
2	ODOM20.ZIP	*Mouse Odometer*, tracks distance of mouse movements
3	OUTLIN.ZIP	Outline control DLL
5	P.ZIP	WAV files starting with P

Chapter	Filename	Description
5	PAISLEY.ZIP	Bitmap image of paisley pattern
5	PARROT1.ZIP	Another bitmap image, can you guess what of?
6	PBBSW32A.ZIP	First file for PowerBBS
6	PBBSW32B.ZIP	Second file for PowerBBS
6	PBBSW32C.ZIP	Third file for PowerBBS
8	PDEMON.ZIP	Drag and drop printing utility for File Manager
5	PEND12.ZIP	*Pendulous*, strategy game like Stratego
5	PERUBMP2.ZIP	Several bitmap images of Peru
6	PLOG1.ZIP	Phone log manager, tracks long distance calls
6	PLOG1-2.ZIP	Second file for the phone log manager
3	PLAWAV.ZIP	Play WAV files with this DLL
4	PLAYCD.ZIP	Another CD player
8	PNR_5.ZIP	*PC News and Report*, Windows edition
6	PRNTVB.ZIP	Print Visual Basic programs
4	PROGMA.ZIP	Program Manager and DDE classes for C++, with source
2	PSPRO201.ZIP	*Paint Shop Pro*, manage many types of graphic images
2	PWBROW.ZIP	Browse program information for EXE, DLL, and VBX files
4	PYRAMD.ZIP	*Pyramid*, solitaire card game with full source
5	Q.ZIP	WAV files starting with Q
5	QCWGAM.ZIP	*Quatra Command*, excellent game
5	R.ZIP	WAV files starting with R
5	RAYWINWP.ZIP	Ray-traced bitmap
5	REDPORSH.ZIP	Another bitmap image from your car wish-list
5	S.ZIP	WAV files starting with S
5	S2.ZIP	More WAV files starting with S

B

Chapter	Filename	Description
8	SAGE20.ZIP	Quote viewer, now with OLE!
2	SCFILE.ZIP	*SCFile*, viewer utility for extra large files
3	SEND.ZIP	Send characters into an application without keystrokes
4	SERIAL.ZIP	Example of Windows program using serial port
4	SETUP2.ZIP	Setup/installation program, with full source
5	SHUTLE1S.ZIP	Bitmap image of the space shuttle in orbit
6	SLSSTP.ZIP	*SLS Setup*, installation program
2	SMARTCAT.ZIP	Disk cataloging program
8	SMTDOC.ZIP	Program to print a complete Help file
3	SPELL2.ZIP	Spelling checker DLL
7	SRGNT.ZIP	Shareware Reference Guide for Windows NT
7	SRGWN.ZIP	Shareware Reference Guide for Windows
4	SS.ZIP	Screen saver with source
4	STKCHK.ZIP	Stack-check memory routines for C programmers
3	SWTOOLS.ZIP	*ShareWare Tools*, helps manage shareware registration collection
5	T.ZIP	WAV files starting with T
8	TASKER.ZIP	Provide toolbar of running applications
2	TC402P.ZIP	*Time & Chaos 4.02*, information manager
3	TEXTVIEW.ZIP	*TextView*, allows simple debugging message management
6	TIMLOG.ZIP	A time logging utility, bill against projects
6	TMBL40.ZIP	A time tracking and billing program
3	TOOLS.ZIP	Utilities for screen design

Chapter	Filename	Description
5	TREK_B.ZIP	Music from commercial breaks for "Star Trek: The Next Generation" and "Star Trek: Deep Space Nine"
2	TTRAK10.ZIP	*TaskTracker*, time tracking manager
5	U.ZIP	WAV files starting with U
7	UNDOC.ZIP	Undocumented Borland C++ tips
8	UNDOCFCT.ZIP	Find undocumented Windows functions
5	V.ZIP	WAV files starting with V
7	VBINDEX.ZIP	List of files in the MS-BASIC area on CompuServe
7	VBKBFT.ZIP	Visual Basic Knowledge Base, from Microsoft
2	VBSYS135.ZIP	Windows system monitor and more
7	VBTIPS.ZIP	*Visual Basic Tips & Tricks* (help file)
7	VBUTL.ZIP	List of Visual Basic files available as shareware or public domain
6	VH.ZIP	*Visual Help*, generates Help files, looks like Visual Basic
5	W.ZIP	WAV files starting with W
5	WALLMAC.ZIP	Bitmap to make your PC look like a Mac
5	WALPAPR1.ZIP	Assorted bitmaps images
5	WALPAPR2.ZIP	More assorted bitmaps
5	WALPAPR3.ZIP	Even more assorted bitmaps
5	WALPAPR4.ZIP	Still more assorted bitmaps
6	WC094.ZIP	*WinCIS*, CompuServe front-end
2	WDIFF.ZIP	Find and show the differences between two ASCII files
4	WDIRLI.ZIP	Windows directory lister, with sizes (and C++ source)
3	WDSM18.ZIP	Windows disassembler
8	WE-30D.ZIP	WinEdit programmer's editor
2	WENV43.ZIP	*Winvelope*, print envelopes with addresses, Postnet barcodes

B

Chapter	Filename	Description
2	WFIND22.ZIP	Win
5	WHOOP.ZIP	*Whoop It Up* ...nds to Windows events
8	WILREL11.ZIP	*WIL Reference*, for use with WinEdit
3	WINDES.ZIP	Data encryption standard DLL
6	WINSET.ZIP	*WinSetup*, installation program
2	WINZIP50.ZIP	*WinZip 5.0*, archive file manager
5	WJ3-0.ZIP	*WinJack*, blackjack game for Windows
6	WNMAIL.ZIP	Windows front-end to the Internet
7	WOLR55.ZIP	*WinOnLine Review*, Issue 55
7	WOLR69.ZIP	*WinOnLine Review*, Issue 69
7	WOLR75.ZIP	*WinOnLine Review*, Issue 75
7	WOLW39.ZIP	*Windows Online "the Weekly,"* Issue 39
7	WOLW40.ZIP	*Windows Online "the Weekly,"* Issue 40
7	WOLW43.ZIP	*Windows Online "the Weekly,"* Issue 43
8	WPOST32B.ZIP	Electronic Post-It™ pad
8	WPRNDIR.ZIP	Add-on for File Manager to print directory lists
6	WPRTSCRN.ZIP	*Print Screen Manager*, allows redirection of screen images
5	WPS100.ZIP	*Win Pelvis-n-Space*, another space game
5	WSAVER.ZIP	A sequence of 14 screen savers for Windows
6	WST40.ZIP	*Windows Set Time*, sets time using government sources
8	WT1.ZIP	First part of WinTune
8	WT2.ZIP	Second part of WinTune
8	WT3.ZIP	Third part of WinTune
5	WT171.ZIP	*Win Trek*, Star Trek game

Chapter	Filename	Description
7	XWINFUN.ZIP	List of files in the Windows FUN area of CompuServe
5	Y.ZIP	WAV files starting with Y
8	YELLOW.ZIP	*Interactive Yellow Pages Network Auction*
5	YTZ110R.ZIP	*Yacht-Z*, just like the original paper Yahtzee
5	Z.ZIP	WAV files starting with Z
5	ZIPAP13B.ZIP	Select bitmaps from compressed files

B

Marketing Your Shareware

How do you make a million bucks in shareware?

Ha, ha. You can't make a million bucks in shareware.

How do you make *some* bucks in shareware?

You can make decent money in shareware if you follow a few simple rules. This is a guide to writing software for money, without the hassle and bother of finding a software publisher.

It's the dream of every programmer: start your own software company, compete with the big boys, break into the market, get treated to trade shows, perhaps get reviewed in *BYTE*...

It never happens. The days of garage-based software companies are waning. To start a software company now, it costs huge amounts of money—from the enormous ad dollars it takes to crack the major publications, to the expensive yet imperative trade shows.

However, if you release your creations as shareware, you're living the entrepreneurial life. You're your own boss. You write the programs you think need to be written. No managers are looking over your shoulders. You get direct feedback from your users. No marketing bozos interfere.

When choosing between two evils, I always like to try the one I've never tried before.
—Mae West

Plus, shareware gets lots of free publicity the big companies can't buy. This is a huge advantage only shareware authors can enjoy.

While working on this and other books, I've talked to countless shareware authors and learned a few of their rules for success. Following them doesn't guarantee great shareware, but they can optimize your shareware's potential.

When it comes to shareware, there is a Golden Rule: Price it seriously, and take it seriously.

For a while, there was a nasty trend of $3 shareware. Some tiny, insignificant program would be let loose on the world, and the author would beg in the About dialog box for a piddling amount of money.

Forget it, folks. No one takes this seriously. Can you really afford to support a program—and no one wants to pay for unsupported software—that makes you $15 a week?

If you write a small program that doesn't do much, and you haven't fully tested it, don't make it shareware. Release it as freeware, or postcardware, or beerware, or whateverware. Just not shareware. When people pay money, they expect results.

Price It Right

How much to charge? Once again, don't ask for too little. Be serious in your effort. Offer a good product, with good support, for a reasonable price. $25 seems to be the average at the moment, although there has been successful shareware at low and high prices.

Generally, I'd recommend $25 for a good, general-purpose utility program. Stick to $25 for even a high-quality game. Go above this amount at your own peril.

Readme the Right Way

Think of the readme file as a voodoo doll. It's the physical manifestation of you, the shareware author, in the hands of the user. Thoughout the book, I've tried to give you a feel for some of the better writing I've found; in your own program,

Look then, into thine heart, and write!
—Henry Wadsworth Longfellow

you become the author, and all eyes are upon you! You get to be cute, witty, knowledgeable, informative, and darned helpful.

But if you're not, your users will poke needles into your eyes. Bad readme files, with inaccurate information, poor instructions, or out-of-date version information, can deaden otherwise glitzy shareware.

Here's a bare-bones sample readme file. Notice that all sorts of important information is included. Feel free to rip off this example. Even if you don't rip off this sample, make sure this information appears in your readmes.

```
[Name] SuperShow



------------------------------------
[Version number] 1.01
------------------------------------
[Copyright notice] Copyright 1994 by John Ribar
------------------------------------
[Contact information]
Internet: jribar@book.net
------------------------------------
[Short description] This program leaps tall
buildings in a single bound...
------------------------------------
[Requirements] Windows 3.1
------------------------------------
[Known incompatibilities] Incompatible with Windows
versions prior to 3.0
------------------------------------
[Installation instructions] Run INSTALL from the
Program Manager
------------------------------------
[How to use] Double-click on the Show icon...
------------------------------------
[Version History] 1.01 - Fixed bug under Windows 3.1
1.0 - First general release.
```

Don't be afraid to let your readme have a friendly, folksy air. People like to read things that have a personal touch. Just don't overdo it. Don't be overly cute. Get to the point—in style, with a little wit and flair.

C

Test Like the Wind

Far too many shareware authors overlook the testing phase. I'm tired of readme files that say things like: "This works on my Gateway, but I heard it may not work on a PS/2." Get real. Test it. Find someone online who can test it for you. Do it. Test on every class of machine. Try different system software versions.

Call the Exterminator

Bug fixes are more important than new features. Get your existing user base working, bug free, before adding bells and whistles. Your reputation will be much better if folks don't crash.

Gentle Prodding versus Cattle Prodding

You need to get paid. How do you ensure that users, who acquire your shareware for free, actually end up paying for it?

Don't tick off your users. Programs that cripple the software—that is, deactivate features until the fee is paid—do poorly.

So how do you make sure you get paid? Shame them into it. You can display a dialog box reminding users to pay every three days. That seems like just the right amount of time; any more, and people will get annoyed. Any less, and they'll forget.

Once users pay, they should be able to disable the reminders. A good way to allow this is to offer some way to enter a registration code into the program.

Tip

GetYour$ is a shareware program in Chapter 3 that performs a lot of the registration, collection, and "make it registered" work for you.

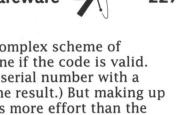

Commercial software often uses a complex scheme of verifying serial numbers to determine if the code is valid. (Usually this is done by XORing the serial number with a large prime number and checking the result.) But making up a special code for each user requires more effort than the average shareware author can afford. Just make up some secret code and have it work for all users. Odds are, people won't share the code. The determined few who really want to crack your program will crack it no matter how sophisticated your code. (Shame on anyone low enough to crack shareware!)

If You Love Something, Set It Free

Once you've written the program, tested it sufficiently, written the readme, and put the whole thing into an archive, you're ready to release it to the world. This can be a scary step. It can also be thrilling. It's exciting to see something of yours online!

Following are a few places you must be sure to upload your creation. Make sure you post it in the appropriate forum and also send it to the forum leader for his or her consideration.

- CompuServe
- GEnie
- America Online
- Prodigy
- Internet (various locations)

Also post it on Delphi, major bulletin board systems, and other e-worlds as you see fit. If you don't have access to any of these, check with friends, local computer stores, or user groups for folks who can post it for you. And check back in Chapter 1 for some phone numbers to get you started.

Post the Notes

Make sure people know about your program. Post notices on all the relevant message boards that your program is available. Tell what it does and how much it costs. List any special features and include any cool comments from your beta testers.

Collecting the Loot

In the end, perhaps only a small percentage of your users will pay you. Yet the easier you make it for them to pay, the more money you will make. Make sure your name and address are clearly visible in both the readme and the opening screen(s). Include an option to print a registration form, or offer fax-based registration service.

CompuServe has a service called SWReg, which charges shareware fees to the user's credit card. This is the easiest way for users to pay. Although CompuServe levies a 15% surcharge, you'll make up for it in registrations. For your shareware to be successful, it's imperative that users be able to register their copies this way.

Don't forget that Uncle Sam wants his cut. The IRS will snag you if you're not careful. Shareware fees are, after all, income, and a whole raft of tax laws deals with money from self-employment, which shareware is.

The Final 10%

Keep up appearances, whatever you do.
—Charles Dickens

Are you the kind of person who responds to customers? Well, you better be, if you want to be successful in shareware. Answer your users' letters. Respond to the comments, both kind and unkind. Make it clear you've heard them, and thank them for their input. That final 10% of the effort—which usually takes 90% of your time—is spent in support. Take the time to do it right.

If your support callers/e-mailers/visitors haven't paid, gently urge them to do so. Remember, sales is a necessary evil in this world. Your e-mail to users will be the closest thing to a sales pitch, besides the actual shareware and readme, you'll ever have. If you hate sales as much as I do, then practice the fine art of the soft sell. Don't be pushy. Be a good, honest, and deserving person. Good things will follow.

Index

More Programming Tools on CDROM!
◆ see next page for detailed product information.

1 Please Fill Out Completely

Shipping Address
Company _____

Name _____

Address/Mail Stop _____

City _____

State/Zip/Country _____

Telephone -- with an Area and Country code.
(in case there is a question about your order)

2 Payment Method

If you are ever unsatisfied with one of our products, simply return the item with your invoice number and a short note saying what is wrong.

◆   Check enclosed. (Drawn on a United States Bank.)

◆   Please charge to my:
❏ Visa   ❏ MC   ❏ Discover   ❏ American Express

Name on Card _____

Cardholder Signature _____

Account # _____

Expiration Date _____

3 I'd Like to Order:

____ x	Hobbes	600 MB current Shareware for OS/2	$ 29.95*	Total $_____
____ x		Subscription: new every 3 months	$ 19.95*/issue	Total $_____
____ x	CICA	4000 new Windows™ programs	$ 29.95*	Total $_____
____ x		Subscription: you get yours first	$19.95*/issue	Total $_____
____ x	Simtel	Classic: 650 MB Shareware for MSDOS	$ 29.95*	Total $_____
____ x		Subscription: quarterly updates!	$19.95*/issue	Total $_____
____ x	Space&Astronomy	Thousands of NASA images and data files	$39.95*	Total $_____
____ x	Giga Games	3000 hot Games for MSDOS & Windows™	$39.95*	Total $_____
____ x	CoC	CDROM of CDROMs -- 4067 descriptions.	$ 39.95	Total $_____
____ x	Libris Britannia	DOS Scientific & Engineering with book	$ 59.95*	Total $_____
____ x	La colección	MSDOS/OS/2/Windows™. Spanish indexes	$ 39.95*	Total $_____
____ x	QRZ!	Ham Radio call sign database + files	$ 29.95*	Total $_____
____ x		Subscription: auto. new every 3 months	$ 19.95*/issue	Total $_____
____ x	Tax Info '93	335 IRS Tax forms & instructions	$ 39.95	Total $_____
____ x	ClipArt	ClipArt Cornucopia -- 5050 images	$ 39.95	Total $_____
____ x	Fractal Frenzy	2000 beautiful high resolution fractals	$ 39.95	Total $_____
____ x	Travel	202 Hi-Res US, Europe travel images	$ 39.95	Total $_____
____ x	GIFs Galore	5000 GIF images - all categories - no adult	$ 39.95*	Total $_____
____ x	Gutenberg	Project Gutenberg: classic literature, docs	$ 39.95	Total $_____
____ x		Subscription: about every 6 months	$ 24.95/issue	Total $_____
____ x	Internet Info	15,000 computer and Internet documents	$39.95	Total $_____
____ x	SysV r4	610 MB ready-to-run Unix Sys V utilities	$ 59.95*	Total $_____
____ x	Nova	600 MB Black Next app's, src., docs, etc.	$ 59.95*	Total $_____
____ x	Nebula	600 MB NeXTSTEP Intel app's, docs, etc.	$ 59.95*	Total $_____
____ x	Aminet	650 MB new files for the Amiga	$ 29.95*	Total $_____
____ x		Subscription: you get yours first	$ 19.95*/issue	Total $_____
____ x	GEMini	616 MB 3000 programs for Atari	$ 39.95*	Total $_____
____ x	Info-Mac	10,000 Mac files from Sumac archive	$ 49.95*	Total $_____
____ x	X11R5 /GNU	X Windows and GNU software for SPARC	$ 39.95	Total $_____
____ x	Source	600 MB Unix & MSDOS source code	$ 39.95*	Total $_____
____ x	CUG	C User Group C source code	$ 49.95*	Total $_____
____ x	Ada	Programming tools, source code and docs	$ 39.95*	Total $_____
____ x	Sprite	Berkeley distributed OS for SUN	$ 29.95	Total $_____
____ x	Linux	Yggdrasil Linux O/S. GNU & X11 src.	$ 49.95	Total $_____
____ x	Toolkit	For Linux - 600 MB util. + Slackware	$ 39.95*	Total $_____
____ x	FreeBSD	Berkeley BSD for PC, w/GNU & X11 src.	$ 39.95	Total $_____
____ x		Subscription: new about every 4 months	$ 24.95/issue	Total $_____
____ x	FAQ	alt.cd-rom Frequently Asked Questions	$ 1.00	Total $_____
____ x	Jewelbox	Clear plastic CD boxes (pack of 10)	$ 5.00	Total $_____
____ x	Caddy	Quality standard caddies — Best Price!	$ 4.95	Total $_____

Shareware requires payment to author if found useful.

Sub-Total $ _____

Tax 8.25%, (California residents only) $ _____

Shipping & Handling ($5 US/Canada, $10 Air Overseas per order) $ _____

Grand Total $ _____

Walnut Creek CDROM
4041 Pike Lane, Suite D-851   Phone: 510 674-0783
Concord CA 94520   Fax: 510 674-0821
USA   Email: orders@cdrom.com

Call 1 800 786-9907

More Programming Tools on CDROM!
CICA Shareware for Windows™ CDROM

"This disc made buying a CDROM drive worth it."
-Steve Wright, Rockville, MD.

$ 29.95

The CICA CDROM disc contains a copy of the Center for Innovative Computer Applications (i.e. CICA). CICA is the Internet's largest Microsoft Windows ftp site, with 600 MB of MS Windows programs. The CICA CDROM's friendly shell makes accessing all these files easy.

With the CICA disc you get hundreds of utilities, including shells, disk utilities, mouse and keyboard utilities, screen savers, backup/restore programs, performance monitors, diagnostics and data conversion programs. The CICA CDROM contains drivers for a large variety of printers and video monitors. You'll also get demos for many commercial Windows programs.

There's plenty of fun stuff on the CICA disc too. You'll find 200 games like asteroids, checkers, chess, word and card games. Liven up your writing with Postscript, ATM, and TrueType fonts. You'll get thousands of icons and dozens of bitmaps to personalize your desktop.

When programming, you'll find the programming tools on the CICA disc vital. There are programming tools for C, C++, Toolbook, Turbo Pascal, and Visual Basic. Many programs include their source code. The CICA CDROM is BBS-ready, with file indexes for opus, RBBS, PCBoard, Wildcat, Maximus, and Spitfire BBS's.

We last updated the CICA disc in December 1993. Shareware progress is rapid so we update this disc *quarterly*. You can be sure you continue to receive the freshest quality shareware with our subscription plan. Order yours today!

Other CDROMs produced by Walnut Creek CDROM include:

Cica MS Windows CDROM	Thousands of programs for MS Windows
Giga Games CDROM	Games for MSDOS and MS Windows
Space and Astronomy CDROM	Thousands of NASA images and data files
C Users Group Library CDROM	A collection of user supported C source code
Simtel MSDOS CDROM	Shareware/Freeware for MSDOS
Clipart Cornucopia CDROM	Clipart for Desktop Publishing
QRZ Ham Radio CDROM	FCC Callsign Database plus shareware
Gifs Galore CDROM	Over 6000 GIF Images
Project Gutenberg CDROM	Classic Literature and historical documents
Hobbes OS/2 CDROM	Shareware/Freeware for OS/2
Source Code CDROM	650 Megabytes of source code for programmers
Internet Info CDROM	Thousands of computer and network documents
X11/Gnu CDROM	X Windows, and Gnu software for Unix and SPARC
Aminet Amiga CDROM	Shareware/Freeware for Amiga
Ada Programming CDROM	Programming tools, Ada source code and docs
Nova for NeXT CDROM	Programs for black NeXT
Nebula for NeXTSTEP Intel CDROM	Programs for NeXTSTEP Intel
Garbo MSDOS/Mac CDROM	MSDOS and Macintosh Shareware/Freeware
Fractal Frenzy CDROM	High resolution images of fractals
FreeBSD CDROM	Complete FreeBSD Operating system, X11R5/GNU
Toolkit for Linux CDROM	Programs and Documentation for Linux OS
GEMini Atari CDROM	Programs for the Atari ST

SEE REVERSE PAGE FOR ORDER INFORMATION

Walnut Creek CDROM

4041 Pike Lane, Suite D-851
Concord CA 94520
Phone   510 674-0783
Fax   510 674-0821
Email   orders@cdrom.com

OR CALL TOLL-FREE
1 800 786-9907

EMPOWERMENT!

BYTE

Shouldn't you be reading BYTE?

The purchase of this book will help you expand your computing skills and know-how. And so will BYTE magazine–in every area of computing!

BYTE gives you the insight needed to do a lot more computing with what you've got. And know a lot more about what you're getting–before you buy.

At BYTE, we believe skills and know-how are the very core of computing power. So we keep you on top of all the latest news. From hot scoops to first-

word briefings on breakthrough products, BYTE delivers state-of-the-art computing intelligence like no other magazine in America.

Articles that compare and evaluate equipment across platforms. Late-breaking reports on advanced technologies. Hardware and software reviews that really appreciate end-user needs. Database, word processor, spreadsheet, and utilities innovations.

And BYTE (unlike most magazines) owes no allegiance to any one operating system, application, vendor, or architecture. For 17 years, BYTE's mission has been to fulfill your need to know the best solutions to challenging computing problems–regardless of brand name, environments of origin, or trend-of-the-month.

Receive your FREE copy of BYTE magazine by returning the coupon below today–Or call 1-800-257-9402 for even faster delivery! Please refer to OSBK012

Your first issue of BYTE is a
FREE ISSUE!

☑ Send me the next issue of BYTE Magazine--FREE! If BYTE is for me I'll return your invoice and pay just $19.97 for 11 more issues (12 in all). If not, I'll write "cancel" on your invoice, return it, and hear no more from you. And the sample copy of BYTE you send will still be mine to keep, ABSOLUTELY FREE!

OSBK012

_____
NAME

_____
COMPANY

_____
ADDRESS

_____
CITY   STATE   ZIP

Basic annual rate: $29.95. Annual Newsstand price: $42.00. Please allow six to eight weeks for delivery of FREE issue.

BYTE · P.O. Box 558 · Hightstown, NJ · 08520

Timely Computing Intelligence
in a Fast-Paced World of Change

Save 53% off the newsstand price for BYTE

(Available only to purchasers of this book!)

If you need to know

   the best solutions…

   the latest thinking…

   the most advanced insight…

regardless of platform, operating systems, application, vendor, or system architecture…

your best bet for timely information is BYTE.

BUSINESS REPLY MAIL
FIRST CLASS MAIL PERMIT NO. 42 HIGHTSTOWN, NJ

POSTAGE WILL BE PAID BY ADDRESSEE:

BYTE
Subscription Department
P.O. Box 558
Hightstown, N.J. 08520-9409

NO POSTAGE
NECESSARY
IF MAILED
IN THE
UNITED STATES